All Scripture references taken from the KJV of the Holy Bible, unless otherwise indicated.

Power Money: Nine Times the Tithe by

Dr. Marlene Miles

Freshwater Press

First printing, 2001

Second printing 2022

ISBN: 978-1-960150-85-1

Copyright 2023 by Dr. Marlene Miles

All rights reserved. No part of this book may be reproduced, distributed, or transmitted by any means or in any means including photocopying, recording or other electronic or mechanical methods without prior written permission of the publisher except in the case of brief publications or critical reviews.

Table of Contents

FOREWORD 4
DON'T SPEND YOUR PRINCIPAL 6
HOW MUCH IS THE PRINCIPAL? 13
YOU CAN'T KEEP THE PRINCIPAL   (AT YOUR HOUSE) 15
HIDDEN TALENTS 19
POWER MONEY 26
YOUR PAY 31
TITHE OR OFFERING 34
THE TITHE IS THE WORD 37
SEED AND INCREASE 45
AGREEMENT 47
INCREASE AND SEED 50
HOW DO I RECEIVE SEED AND INCREASE? 53
RECOGNIZE THE TITHE 56
HOW DOES THE TITHE RETURN VOID? 65
WHAT IS THE WORD? 70
YOU CAN'T KEEP THE TITHE AT YOUR HOUSE 72
A WELL-TUNED INSTRUMENT 76
NINE TIMES THE TITHE 81
WHAT IF YOU HAVE BECOME POWERLESS? 86
BEING IN THE RIGHT PLACE AT THE RIGHT TIME 91
YOUR FINANCIAL PORTFOLIO 99
10 TIMES THE TITHE 101
WHO ARE YOU? 107
THE 10 COMMANDMENTS OF THE TITHE 109
THE 10 COMMANDMENTS OF TITHING 111
EPILOGUE 116

CHRISTIAN BOOKS BY THIS AUTHOR 117

Power Money

Nine Times the Tithe

Freshwater Press

Foreword

The concept of the Tithe will be explored in this book in a new and revelatory way that you may not have been exposed to. This information has been described as *deep*; but there are more levels to God than most of us take time to pursue and fully understand. I feel that God challenges me, and I, in turn, challenge you to strong meat. We know that God loves us, and that's comforting, but that is the sincere milk of which Paul speaks. On a deeper level, let's find out *how much* God loves us and how He has set things in motion for us to experience the depth of His care.

The word, *Word* is capitalized in this book to indicate the Word of God. The word, Tithe is capitalized to indicate the noun, *Tithe*, which is the money used in the act of tithing. Any other times, these words are capitalized it is to emphasize their importance to you, your living, and the revelation of **Power Money:** *Nine Times the Tithe.*

The word, *tithe*, when not capitalized will speak of the *act* of tithing, the verb, *to tithe.*

As you partake of this strong meat, I pray the Holy Spirit will be alongside you to minister the message of **Power Money: Nine Times the Tithe** to your full understanding and transform your financial status, as God transforms you to be more like Christ, more like His heir.

For as the heavens are higher than the Earth, so are my ways higher than your ways, and my thoughts than your thoughts.

For as the rain cometh down, and the snow from heaven, and returneth not thither, but watereth the earth, and maketh it bring forth and bud, that it may give seed to the sower, and bread to the eater:

So shall my word be that goeth forth out of my mouth: it shall not return unto me void, but it shall accomplish that which I please, and it shall prosper in the thing whereto I send it.

Isaiah 55:9-11

Don't Spend Your Principal

A retired man began to teach the concept of the *Principal* to his also retired wife. After three years of instruction, she said she understood. That same year, he died. She began to receive the just over $4,000 per month dividend (interest) checks that he had been receiving from their investments and using in their retirement. He had set up their life's savings and inheritance from both of their parents in a way to make the money work for them, and not exhaust the *Principal*. He had not withdrawn any of the money they had invested over the years; that was the *Principal*. By leaving the *Principal* invested he provided the way to bless himself and his wife. And, because the *Principal* was preserved, their three grown children would also benefit after the parents had passed on. The children would receive the principal as part of their inheritance, along with life insurance benefits.

Immediately after his death, the widow became eager to handle the money--, all of it, as it was something she always wanted to do. Her first action was to withdraw all the money which was earning close to 10% interest out of three different large accounts because it now *belonged* to her. Perhaps there was a sense of insecurity; her husband had taken care of all the finances through their 40-year marriage, but now he was gone. It was as though she wanted to be surrounded by *her* money. It could be that she was grieving and not thinking clearly. Perhaps she never really understood the teachings of her husband on the *Principal*. Maybe she was just plain greedy; but she was planning to put several hundred thousand dollars in her non-interest-bearing checking account. I suppose she thought that would make her feel more assured, or even rich to have all that money at her fingertips. Ridiculous, as the FDIC does not even insure deposits as large as she was going to be placing in a checking account. And, a checking account, whether it pays interest or not, is s not the wise place for that large of a sum of money. A checking account is never the place for *Principal* that should be invested.

She was stopped before she made this grievous error.

It is human nature to want to get what is yours. Too many want to withdraw retirement, pensions, annuities, or savings. Too many want to go and get it --, all of it. Insecurity and lack of faith causes people to go get what is theirs, prematurely. People may not have faith in banks or other money institutions, and therefore do not trust that the money will be there when they want or need it. Or, the investor does not know or learn the rules, laws and regulations of money-making and money management. Instead, they do not invest at all, or they may withdraw or move money, making regrettable mistakes.

Closing those accounts would have removed the money-making *Principal* that paid those regular checks that the couple had been living on. Shutting down those accounts for whatever reason, would have shut down the *vehicle* that was put in place to bless that widow woman. Withdrawn money creates cash on hand, but unless reinvested, it will not be working to draw more money to itself. And, if you do not reinvest it quickly, you may have to pay penalties for having taken it out in the first place.

Every financially well off or rich person knows this hard and fast rule of finances: **Don't spend your Principal.** It is the first rule of successful financial economics. If you desire to be well off, or even rich, don't spend your *Principal*. If you are wise, you will not spend your Principal. Prosperous parents teach their children this very early in life and they make sure their children understand. Don't spend your *Principal.*

Don't spend your *Principal* means don't spend the money that's making you money. Don't get rid of or lose the source of your increase. Don't kill the goose that's laying the golden eggs. It's akin to *Don't bite the hand that's feeding you.* Don't close savings accounts that are paying you interest. Don't withdraw money from stock accounts, mutual funds, pensions, IRA's, 401K's, and other retirement accounts until it's time.

If you have investments or savings that earn you a dividend or interest check, the money that is invested is your *Principal*. Principal is not disbursements from such as annuities or money you already own that you are receiving over time. It is not the monthly payments from a legal settlement. Neither is it your Social Security benefits.

Money that you're just receiving could be your regular paycheck, bonuses, royalties, cash prizes, earnings, and winnings. You may be collecting these awards over a period of time. Money can't work for you as *Principal* until it's invested, and small amounts cannot work efficiently until you invest it with other money. Money that is already set up in accounts in your name is *Principal*, and the money it earns may be called interest, dividends, or capital gains. Invested *Principal* is money that you already own, that you either deposited yourself, incrementally over time, or all at once.

Principal could be money you've earned, or money given to you as a gift or an inheritance, for example. Or, it could be a combination of money from different sources. Once this money is invested and some time period has passed, it begins to make money for you--, not just a little interest here and there that is redeposited or reinvested, but it creates substantial money that you can receive without touching the *Principal*. This money can be called dividends. Dividend payments are sizable and can be sent to you on regular intervals as you establish or agree to. Many retirees live off the payments from these types of investments. I'm not talking about Social Security. I'm talking about a very large amount of your own money invested in some way that makes money for you and pays you dividends.

For example, if you are receiving a dividend check of $1000 per month from an investment, you can never withdraw the money that makes up that investment if you want to keep receiving the $1000 each month; that is the *Principal*. Withdrawing the Principal will stop the monthly checks. The *Principal* is invested money in those accounts that is causing you to receive the $1000 per month. If you withdraw, decrease or alter the amount of the *Principal*, you stop, decrease, or alter the amount of your monthly payment. You will receive less, based on how much is left in your account to earn interest dividends, or capital gains. Don't forget the penalties for withdrawing the *Principal* in the first place, especially if you don't put it back in place with timeliness.

Another very wealthy older woman, using Wisdom and discretion, told the man whom she was about to marry, *"We can spend all the interest and dividends off my investments that we want. We can really enjoy ourselves, but I love my children and I'm leaving them the Principal."*

That woman may have inherited *Principal* from her parents and therefore learned to preserve, protect, and pass it on. She could have earned it and saved it herself. You don't have to inherit *Principal* to have *Principal*, but you have to have discipline to amass *Principal* if you aren't given any. And, you have to be taught, study, or get teaching on how to manage the *Principal* that you are blessed to have if you want it to work for you. Use Wisdom whenever you do anything with the *Principal*.

If you don't have any Principal, of course, your goal is to get some; save it, or borrow it. Borrowing the Principal is usually only justified if you are very young and/or if you make a very large annual salary. If you are searching for the perfect gift to give your children, or anyone you love, give them *Principal*. If you had disciplined parents who really understood money, they gave or left you, *Principal*.

If you've waited too late in life, you may be one of those who has just saved up enough money off of which to live in your retirement. That's better than having no money at all, but it's not the best way. Living off interest or dividends or invested *Principal* and being able to leave that *Principal* to your children, (Proverbs 13::22b) is the better way, and pleases God.

The *Principal*, which is money, attracts more money to itself. Growing and managing Principal properly can lead to and assure prosperity. When the dividends from the *Principal* are not paid out, but reinvested, the *Principal* can grow dramatically. If you can afford to have your dividends reinvested, do it. In gambling circles that is called *letting it ride*. Gambling is not God's way, but I mention it here as an example of leaving what is invested in place as you wait (or hope) for more increase.

Your financial Principal in conventional accounts, such as stocks, bonds, mutual and other funds can grow as well. They can double, triple, or increase multiple times if the investment is left in place, over time. This is the process by which retirement and college fund accounts work. Many deposits have been added and compounded with interest and dividends to make a very large investment that will pay monthly or quarterly checks. If these checks are large enough, you can live on them as your primary income or enjoy a supplemental income in your *golden years*. In that way, you preserve the *Principal* and then you're able to pass that nest egg, or *Principal* on to your heirs.

The *Principal* is a powerful sum of money invested for you to receive increase. The word *Principal* will not be italicized in subsequent chapters.

How Much Is the Principal?

It can take a lifetime to build a sizable Principal, although some spend a lifetime spending would-be Principal one week, one dollar, one paycheck at a time. When the time comes, they have no nest egg to live on or to pass on to their children. To most people, the Principal is only as much as they can afford. Often it is only as much or as little as they have the discipline to invest and leave in the account. That's the truth. But, unfortunately, many have not exercised the discipline to deposit funds into nest eggs, retirement and other accounts as they should.

Too many are living on money that they should be investing, either because of need, greed, lack of discipline, they have no vision for the future, but just want to live large today. Living on the money that should be designated for the *golden years* is not wise, because it's not yet *golden* money. It is only a little bit, right now. It doesn't get *golden* until it's invested and multiplies. Then, it's right for the *golden* years.

The Principal should be as much as possible. You should have a certain minimum goal and if you surpass that--, great. You do this by deciding that you want to receive X number of dollars per week, month, quarter, or year from your Principal, when you start receiving checks. You do not start receiving checks when you are growing your investment. Growth occurs when you let your interest and dividends rollover, become reinvested; when you let it *ride*.

Most people don't begin to receive checks until retirement or partial retirement.

Now that you understand the Principal, all you have to do is figure out how much Principal you need to have in place when you start receiving checks, based on the interest rate, to supply the desired or needed weekly, monthly, or quarterly check amount that will sustain or enhance your living.

Principal X Interest Rate =

Amount of Dividend Check

Remember, some period of time must pass. By deciding how much or what percentage of your current earnings will go into your retirement or other investment accounts and doing it you can create and grow the amount of principle that you need and desire.

Now you can see why you studied Algebra in high school--, for your real life. If you have money and plan to have and handle money successfully, you need to know Algebra.

You Can't Keep the Principal (At Your House)

Once the Principal is invested, if it's going to work for you, it must stay invested. It must stay in the place where it will do it's work, which is attracting more money to itself. Spoiled or disobedient children, gamblers, lottery winners, widows and widowers who don't really understand money are notorious for removing the Principal and wasting the money that people have left them, or given them.

The greedy have a very difficult time working this principle because they want to spend the money today for immediate gratification. They don't have patience or faith to wait for the Principal to prosper itself and become a money-making investment that will sustain them. The greedy need teaching and discipline, so that prosperity, and in some cases, deliverance will come to overcome avarice, covetousness, and fear so they can work the principles of money and successfully live.

Many lottery winners and gamblers may not understand the laws of money. Their only law is luck and there is no such law. They believe that money is *just money,* and they don't **recognize** the Principal. All they really know and sometimes care about is that they win. There is a charge, a demonic rush to win in gambling--, it affects the very soul. Additionally losing in gambling brings on a strong, addictive soul response as well. Often gamblers only know that they have finally been given money, and many times, lots of it!

Easy come, easy go; they don't recognize or care that part of, or all of this money should be set aside as Principal. They respond to the urge to bet it again based on a feeling or a desire for things, stuff, more money for the rush of winning. That's why most lottery and sweepstakes winners are broke again very soon after winning.

Not recognizing the Principal is how it gets lost, stolen, or spent. People who remove the Principal from the position of working for them and put it in wrong places or spend it, shut up Heaven and diminish or shut off their blessings or prosperity. They risk penalties and losses as a result. Without the Principal, no interest will be accrued. Without the Principal there will be no dividends or capital gains. Without Principal, there will be no increase. No Principal means no interest, no gains, no dividends, no increase, which means no payments and no checks.

If you have thousands of dollars but it's not invested anywhere, there is no Principal; it's *only money*, and it won't make you any money. When you take it out of the place of being Principal and put it in your checking account or in your hot little hands, you diminish it, and demote it to *just money*. You must recognize the Principal and keep it in it's place. It will thrive and draw more money to itself if it is Principal. If it is *just money*, it will only pay a few bills, buy you a car, or a few disposable things such as clothes, and then vanish. Poof!

You'll be laughed at like so many gamblers, lottery winners, spoiled children, undisciplined workers, and undereducated widows, asking the same question, *"What happened to all that money?"* When it was demoted from being the Principal it lost it's **power** to prosper. If it's not assigned the responsibility of being Principal, it remains as *only money*--, just mundane, run-of-the -mill money.

I am in no way saying to worship money especially since I've spoken so highly of Principal money. **Do not worship money**. Instead, put money to work for you. Principal money works for you; mundane everyday money does not, it's *only money*. **YOU** work for mundane money.

Just money, *only money* and simply money or whatever you choose to call it does not have the ability that Principal money has to attract more money to itself. And the more Principal money you have, the more money it will attract to itself. Larger Principals draw higher interest rates than smaller amounts, in the very same type of account; however, d*espise not small beginnings.*

Invested Principal draws money to itself; uninvested money does not. The bigger, the better. So let it grow.

Time is money. Money that's committed to stay invested long term draws more interest. Even large amounts won't have a good return if not left there the proper amount of time. Leave it where it can grow.

Despise not small beginnings. A fruit tree that can feed a lot of people starts out only as seed, but over time there's much fruit. Your little nest egg that you're growing into Principal can be passed on from generation to generation to feed lots of people in your family.

Hidden Talents

Or the Principal can all be withdrawn and hidden in mattresses or shoeboxes. It can be hoarded up or squandered, dwindling away day by day. Much that should be invested is not, but instead spent right away on everyday stuff.

Once it is moved from its position of Principal, the real gamble is on. Will the money last as long as you do, or will you outlast it? Or, have you timed things perfectly, so you and the money expire together? It takes a lot of calculation and planning to be that selfish, unless you have zero heirs. Don't you want to leave anything to anyone? Your children? Yes? -- for the work that should go on after you're gone. If you withdraw the Principal, you will begin to spend it. And more like sooner than later, even large amounts of money will disappear.

Withdrawn money will not work the principle of money attracting money and the Principal (the money itself) will not work for you. Neither will God's principle of **Nine Times the Tithe** work when you withdraw the Tithe or keep it in your pockets or your hot little hands. When you spend the Tithe it's as though the rest of that money just runs through your fingers or disappears-- , even large amounts.

God's Tithe also does not work in your checking, savings, IRA, mutual fund, or any of our personal accounts. It only works when it's put back in its proper place: the tithing envelope and offering basket of your church. The Principal works to attract interest, create dividends, or to compound and multiply; that's when money is doing what it should be doing. Unexposed, hidden shoebox funds do not work Godly principles, and that does not please God. That includes money that should be designated as ***Tithes*** and offerings but is not.

Look at the Parable of the Talents (Matthew 25:25-28). Here, *Talents* is not interpreted literally; it is not singing skills, drum playing or tap dancing. A Biblical Talent was money; if made of gold, a Talent was worth about $30,000. If of silver, a Talent was worth about $2000.

In the parable, God chose three servants. He *fronted* them all Talents, (money) based on their several abilities, which we can infer as their faith, acumen, willingness, spiritual, and natural talents, gifts, and skills. God gave this money to them with the expectation of both a report and return of the money.

And, He expected that the money would be put to work and that it would cause an increase.

Nobody spent the money. Nobody lent or gave it to a friend or family member. I believe they recognized it was from God. Here's a good place to ask yourself, where do you think the money that you live on comes from? The government? The US Mint? Fort Knox? Yes, on Earth. But God commands the blessing of money to come to you. Man just decides the currency. God also creates the *material* of which the currency is made, whether it's salt, shells, silver, paper, plastic, or gold--, God created it all. Man has neither created money, nor the stuff of which it is made.

Those who believe that money is the paper it's printed on are just a step away from becoming forgers. Those who believe that money is the paper, the silver, or the gold that we call *money* can easily leave God out of the whole transaction. That's why God told us not to create idols, not of gold, silver, paper, or anything. Don't make an idol of money, and don't make the stuff that money is made of into an idol.

In the Parable of the Talents, they also understood that they had to give an account for this money as when someone gives or lets you use something with the expectation of seeing it again. What's that called? *Borrowed.* Since God expected to see this money again, we know that He *lent* it to them.

God doesn't do things without purpose; so, He lent them the money with a purpose. The purposes may have been to help and or teach them.

In his investing, the servant with the two Talents made a total of four talents. The servant that had five talents also doubled his startup amount to end up with 10 talents. The 5 Talents went out and multiplied *after its kind,* to make 10.

The servant who hid his talent ended up with the same amount he started with-, one. He hid that talent, which was the Principal, his startup money in the Earth, which is the same as stashing money in the side compartment of your wallet or other secret place. Jesus called the servant who hid the Principal, *wicked,* (Matthew 25). He had everything taken away from him since that was not pleasing to God. He had an excuse though, as most do. He was afraid that he'd lose it; and he did. But, even the wicked servant knew not to lose or give away that which is God's. Hiding or keeping it at your house doesn't please God; that's considered wicked.

The faithful servant who multiplied 5 talents into ten was very pleasing to God.

God gives to each of us a measure of faith, and according to our *several abilities,* 10 talents. Not necessarily the cash equivalent of Biblical Talents, which would have been about $60,000 to $150,000 if the talents were of gold, and about $4000 to $10,000 if the Talents were in silver. But for the purposes of this book, God gives us some *startup money*, some *front money* for our spiritual investing and the startup money is the **Tithe**. God has *fronted* us all with the Tithe. That is the reason to rejoice right there.

God expects His Tithe back; so, you could think of the Tithe as a loan.

Where is this *front money*?

Well, you get it by faith at the beginning of the week, but you don't see it tangibly until after it has worked hard for you. It shows up in places like your paycheck, gifts, rewards, bonuses, winnings, and blessings--, it shows up *in* your money.

If you're faithful with what God starts you out with, He increases the *Talents*, the startup or stake money--, the Tithe amount.

Unfortunately for the unfaithful in money, here we see the work of the Devourer. God allows the Devourer to take money and things of value from the unfaithful, just as it was taken away from the wicked in the parable. When you consider the vast numbers of professed Christians, whom God may have *fronted* Tithe money, then the numbers who have been unfaithful in the Tithe, then you'll realize that disobedience to God's laws has caused a lot of Talents to be confiscated.

When the Tithe is not paid back, the Devourer can come in and get it.

Where is this confiscated money?

Laid up. The wealth of the wicked is laid up for the *just*. The wicked are the unsaved, but who else did Jesus call wicked? Those who did not prosper with what God has given them.

So, the wealth of the wicked is laid up. Does the Devourer have it? No. Even though he sticks his greedy nose in, ultimately **what is God's goes back to God.** God has it laid up waiting to be transferred to the righteous. Who are the righteous? The righteous are not the church members who come every Sunday necessarily. Nor are they the ones who volunteer when asked to do church assignments, necessarily. They are not the ones who have been on Church Roll longest, necessarily. They may, and should do all of those things, but the righteous in this case are the faithful Tithers. There is a lot of increase out there to be gained by the faithful.

The wealth of the wicked is laid up for the just --, just the Tithers (Proverbs 13:22b). Those who have hidden the Tithe have also laid it up for God to recover and give to the just – just the Tithers. Just us. Just the faithful servants. The wealth of the wicked is laid up for the *Just*.

Who are the *Just*?

The Tithers, just the Tithers. The Just are those who are faithful with the little, with whatever God gives them. They are faithful with money and increase. The *Just* are those who know how to put money in other resources to work for them. They know how to use and prosper what God entrusts to them. And the Just live by faith, (Romans 11:7). Believe me, it takes faith to be a tither.

The Tithe is a most convenient and clever way to transfer wealth. Prosperity and wealth are zipped up in the Tithe. In this way wealth is:

- Transferred to the faithful--, those with discernment to receive this thing of great value, the Tithe or startup money.
- Great wealth can be transferred quickly.
- Transferred only to God's children.
- Double tested.

Are you saved? Are you tithing? God's faithful children who tithe are the ones on the receiving end. It's a great reward and it is transferred right under the enemy's nose. There's nothing the enemy can do about it.

Knowing this, are you a bit more inspired? Are you faithful or unfaithful? What about tomorrow? Which will you be? Faithful, I pray.

POWER MONEY

The Tithe is God's first instrument of your prosperity. Your repenting of not paying the Tithe if you've been disobedient is your first step to prosperity. Until you learn how to work the Tithe, offerings will not work for you, and other blessings will not come to you. And, if you want obedient children, release a *spirit of obedience* in your home by obeying the Word as it pertains to tithing.

In the investment world, the Principal is the money that makes or draws the interest to itself. The interest does not **make** the Principal, although it can add to it. It is the Principal that makes the interest.

The Principal attracts money, but in the natural, that can be a slow process. It can take a lifetime, in some cases, to grow to the size we desire. That's why we should start college funds at the birth of our children and retirement funds as soon as we get jobs.

In the world, the Principal is the lump sum and the interest is the lesser amount that adds to that lump sum to make it grow If you have a nest egg of $10,000 for example, chances are that the $9000 was the

Principal and the $1000 was the interest or dividends, over time, that created that $10,000 grand total.

In the world's economy, it would usually take a very, very long time for $1000 to turn into $10,000, legally. In God's economy $1000 could turn into $10,000 very easily and surprisingly very quickly, and in a spiritually and civilly legal way.

The Tithe, which is only 10%, may seem like too much to pay, if you're selfish, disobedient, greedy and don't want to pay it. But the Tithe is to be paid regularly, and faithfully. What do you think about 10% making 100%? An investment that multiplies itself 10X is a great opportunity.

In the natural, investing $1000 to cause $10,000 to come to you legally will excite both the average and the avid investor, although it could take a while. But in God's economy, I challenge your thinking and understanding today that an investment of $1000 can give you a return of $10,000 very quickly.

When?

When the $1000 is the Tithe.

When $1000 is your Tithe, and you pay it, you're pretty much guaranteed to receive $10,000 in your next paycheck or business earnings. I'm not speaking of arbitrarily taking large sums of money to the church to use the offering basket and God as a casino, Ponzi, or lottery game. The Tithe is designated as 10% of increase that you have already received. It's 10%, but because you have already received your increase, you know how much 10% of your increase is.

The economy of God works differently than the world's system. God's system is better and more efficient. The world's Principal is like God's Tithe in a sense. As the worlds' principal attracts little bits, or even lots of interest to itself, in God's system the Tithe is collecting nine more like itself to itself for your prosperity. In God's system one collects nine just like itself to make 10. The Tithe of only 10% is what **makes** the 100%.

In God's economy, the 10% ($1000) attracts the 90% ($9,000) to make 100% ($10,000). In the world, the Principal attracts 10%, on a good day, to help you prosper. See how God's got it, hands down.

How does the Tithe collect 90% when it's only 10%? It is as though the Tithe grows back to wholeness. I challenge you that the $1000 Tithe caused the $10,000 to come into existence or manifestation, and because you tithe, that is what cause it to come to you.

And it doesn't take as long as it takes a piece of coal to become a diamond, either.

It's not simply that you are making the $10,000 and having to give $1000 to God, or to your church. As you receive *increase*, remember **you** didn't cause the $10,000 to come to you. You didn't earn it, even though you were at your job. **The Tithe of $1000 caused it. You became the recipient at the next increase because you paid the Tithe back to God**. You have just become a partaker of the Divine Nature of God. The Divine Nature of God is, seeds, tithes, everything really reproduces after their own kind. You have just received *increase* from money that reproduced after its own kind because you paid the Tithe. You just participated in the Divine Financial plan of God.

Granted, a $10,000 increase may come to you as your paycheck, merit bonus, or some other form of remuneration, but **it has to appear as something that you know, or you won't receive or accept it** unless you have a very strong measure of the gift of faith. Then, because of the promises of God, because you tithe, the Devourer is rebuked, for your sake (Malachi 3:10) and you can enjoy your increase.

The Tithe is **Power Money**. It has power. The Tithe is what makes the other 90% **come to it**, not the other way around. The world's Principal of $9000 is drawing a little interest, comparatively, to itself, in the previous example to finally, someday, far in the future add up to $10,000. But with God the 90% is not drawing the Tithe to it, the 10% is doing the drawing. The Tithe is drawing money to itself.

Power Money: Nine Times the Tithe is written to prove this to you. Read on.

Important: The principle of Power Money: Nine Times the Tithe works for saved folk who are faithful tithers. It is part of God's plan for our prosperity; it is not a get rich quick scheme. You cannot pretend to be saved or pretend to tithe just to see if this works.

Your faith may not be built up to the level to bring in the increase you want in the time frame that you want. You have to be committed and faithful for God's principles to work for you, and they work by faith in His timing, or by the timing of your faith. As stated, this is part of God's plan for your life and godliness, prosperity, and wealth.

YOUR PAY

Your paycheck of $1000 includes God's $100 Tithe in it. But God doesn't get the Tithe because you made $1000. No, God isn't getting a part of your money. Once again, it's not about you, Baby. You're not the Creator and Sustainer of the whole Earth; God is. You are not making money for God. You are not God's sustainer, He is yours. You're not Jehovah Jireh the Lord, my Provider; God is. It's all about **God.** You're getting blessed because of *His* money, not the other way around.

Remember **God's Grace** and His goodness toward us. God doesn't owe us anything. We are by nature the debtors. That's one reason that the Tithe is **paid**, because it is owed. But, in spite of our debtor nature, by Grace we are the recipients, as God gives us what we don't even deserve. By Grace, God allows us to use the Tithe to cause increase to come to us. God's Tithe or $100 is the reason you are holding the $1000 paycheck in your hand right now. Your job and paycheck are not the reason for the Tithe. **The Tithe is the reason for the job and the paycheck.** That's because the Tithe attracts and multiplies after *its own kind*. The Tithe went out and did the work. Yes, you went to the office, factory, warehouse, or wherever you work, but the Tithe is the reason that you are holding that $1000 paycheck right now.

The Tithe on $1000 is $100. The other money, the $900 in your paycheck, even though it's more (90%), is *only money*. It won't draw, multiply, or do anything unless and until the Tithe is paid. It will just lie in your wallet or pocket, rest on your dresser, or between the mattrass and box springs where you've hidden it. Hidden money is *just money* until the Tithe is paid. The 90% is not Power Money unless:

1. The Tithe is paid and,
2. After the offering money is sown.

When receiving increase, we collect 10 times the Tithe, but after paying the Tithe, the week of receiving the increase, you will still have 9X the Tithe left for living and giving. **Nine Times the Tithe is prosperity**. It's the most you can receive legally from paying the tithe regularly and generously. It opens up a very incredible door to **The Fold**, which is another whole book. **The Fold** is about God's 30-, 60-, and 100-fold increase in your offerings.

Nine Times the Tithe is another way of saying you get to keep 90% of all your increase. It is not the formula for paying and receiving from the Tithe. God will do what He says He will do concerning the Tithe and according to your faith. As far as paying the Tithe (Malachi 3:10), God promises to do the following:

- Rebuke the Devourer for your sake.
- Open the windows of Heaven.
- Pour you out a blessing that's more than enough – and El Shaddai type blessing.
- Your vine will not cast fruit before season.

God can prosper you more or less depending on:

- Your several abilities
- What you start out with,
- Faith and Faithfulness
- Ability to receive, et. cetera.

Nine Times the Tithe is not the formula for making God do anything. It is the formula for identifying and appreciating what you have in your hand after God blesses you. And it's a goal for your faith so you can be the Just. Remember the wealth of the wicked will be transferred to the Just. If you're not tithing, if you're not sowing, if you're not using faith, you're not counted among the Just.

Tithe or Offering

Paying the tithe is one of, if not the *first* instruments of your prosperity. That many people don't use it. Not using it can be detrimental to your financial health. It's not optional because the Bible says it's not. We all know saved people who don't tithe whose paychecks go down to 9X what they do tithe. Many lose very good jobs and opportunities. Many have no jobs at all after a while. I've told you the Tithe is the reason for the job and the paycheck, not the other way around.

It is the money that you paid designated as the Tithe that brings sustained increase of 9X the Tithe.

If you don't yet tithe. But still, have a job and increase, **Grace** is the reason. God is giving you time to deal honestly in your finances.

Speaking of the Tithe and being sustained, we consider the little widow woman at Zarephath, (I King 7:9). She fed the prophet **first**, and *first,* speaks of the Tithe. This woman and her son, which speaks of her generations, were sustained throughout the time of famine. What does famine have to do with us? When we consider the opulence, wealth and riches Jesus left in glory, we should have a certain respect that He became poor, that we might become rich, (2 Corinthians 8:9). As we acknowledge what he left in Heaven is also ours by covenant. No matter what kind of money or wealth we are looking at in the natural, it's as financial famine compared to His riches in Glory. So, the Tithe is first and sustains you while you are here on Earth, and famine compared to what awaits you in eternity.

In offerings, God says He will give some 30-, some 60- and some 100-fold return. God can prosper you more or less in the offering according to your faith and other criteria. The tithe sustains and sets the stage for the offering to make you wealthy. Offerings prosper you to wealth and great wealth.

The Tithe has power. The Principal has *attraction*. The Principal is very attractive to interest. dividends and capital gains. You want some of that attractive Principal money, don't you? In the world, average, everyday money when invested in savings accounts. IRA's. KEOGHS 401K's Stocks. Bonds. Mutual funds. Bitcoin, and the like become Principal. And it's got the ability to attract money to itself and set you up for wealth.

But in God's Kingdom. The Tithe has **POWER**. It is an instrument that God has designed to serve you. Serving you means going out and creating, drawing and causing wealth to come to you for sustaining your life and godliness. The Tithe is a mechanism set in place to serve you. Offerings also serve you, but more about that in the book **The Fold**. God uses what looks like *everyday money*, but when God authorizes it to work on your behalf, it becomes powerful. Working the Tithe is the beginning of prosperity. The offering is the beginning of wealth. You should want as much Tithe as God will trust you with, because that sets the stage for how much you will have left to sow in the offering for the riches that God wants you to have.

The Tithe Is the Word

The sower sows the word, (Mark 4:14)

Most people have at least one Bible in their home. Whether it's used as the Word of God, or an *objet d'art* is another story. Bringing the Good Book out for your Christmas decor is not using the Bible correctly. As with the church, it's not the building, it's the people in it. And it's not just the people in it, it's the life and anointing of the people in the church. The same goes for the Bible. It's not the Book, it's the words in the book. But it's not just the words in the book, it's the life and anointing of the words that are in it. If the words aren't alive or aren't given life, if they are not sown, if they are not spoken, they are only words.

And with money, it's not the paper it's on, or the silver or the gold that's backing it up. It's how the money is used that determines its power and its value. A person who has money may seem to have power, but the person who *sows* money is **more** powerful. When it is sown, money has great potential. Else it's *only money*. But it must be sown properly. You do not sow fish into the air, birds into dirt, or seeds into the water. The Tithe has a place where it will work effectively, else it is not the Tithe, it is *only money*.

The Word **must** be sown and becomes powerful when it is sown. We can sow the Word by speaking it over ourselves, our loved ones, and our lives. But the Word of God is even more powerful when **He** sows it, because it's *His* Word.

When you speak your own word instead of sending it by two or three people, doesn't it have more impact and power? When you tell your little boy to come in out of the rain, does it carry more weight than if you tell his younger sister to tell him? Isn't he more likely to obey that word from you than her? Of course. It's no different with God's Word. It was designed to obey Him. Don't be dismayed. It was also designed to obey those who have Christ's Spirit in them and those who walk in the authority of it. Your daughter's authority may be questioned by your son, evidenced by him responding to his sister, *You're not the boss of me.* But God's Word, when spoken by you with and in authority, should cause many things to happen.

Still, some words that come from the mouth of God can **only** come from the mouth of God. There are still mysteries that we do not know. Some words have to and **must** come from God's mouth. Still, other words don't work in Earth until we **agree** with God.

And God says His Word will accomplish that which He pleases (Isaiah 55:11).

Here we begin to recognize and understand the Tithe. The Tithe is the Word. The sower sows the Word. The Word is a seed. We know from Genesis that all things in God's system reproduce *after their kind*, especially seeds. The Tithe reproduces *after its own kind* also. But how can that be? Only if it's the Word.

After its kind, (Genesis 1:7). Are seeds like sons after their fathers, disciples after Jesus, the little boy's lunch and anointed words. These all reproduce *after their kind*. The little boy's lunch, Yes, fishes and loaves also reproduce *after their kind.* They did for Jesus, both in the water, (Luke 5:4-11), and after they were cooked. *After its kind* is not just for plants, flowers, birds and people. Everything that God made that reproduces follows this law. The fishes and loaves were more of a first fruits than a Tithe, because the little boy gave all, he gave his entire lunch, but it's a good *after its kind* example.

What works in the Earth spiritually to cause multiplication? The Word. So, the Tithe must be an anointed, spoken Word.

So shall my word be that goes forth out of my mouth. It shall not return unto me void, but it shall accomplish that which I please, and it shall prosper in the thing where to I sent it, (Isaiah 55:11).

God also says that His Word will not return to Him **void**. That statement implies that His Word <u>**will**</u> return to Him. If you look in the Scriptures, you will see that the Word has always returned to God. Jesus was the personification of that. Jesus is the Logos; He is the Word. He came to Earth for a season and with purpose, and He accomplished just what He came here to do--, redemption of sinful mankind. Jesus was the Word clothed in flesh. The Word of God was, is, and shall be fulfilled and prospered in the thing that God sends it to accomplish. Even if the Word of God has to go through Hell, it will accomplish what it was sent to do. Jesus did just that. He went through Hell to accomplish His Earthly assignment. After performing its task, the Word will return back to the one who sent it. It will return to God just as Jesus has done. The Word of God is faithful and true, and it can be trusted to do whatever God has sent it to do.

The Tithe's assignment is to behave as the Word, because it is the Word, it collects nine more just like itself to itself, then returns to God.

How does that happen? Think of a magnet that is actually money or money that has become as a magnet. We will use a $100 bill that's been spiritually magnetized by God for this example. That's what I'm calling the *Tithe magnet*. The magnet draws to itself others that look just like it. And since we're in the economy of God and it's the 10th, the Tithe, it will attract nine other $100 bills to itself, just like itself. The tithe magnet reproduces ***after its kind***, giving a total of ten $100 bills, or $1000. The original $100 bill, which is the Tithe, doesn't look any different than the others, but it behaves differently. It behaves as the Word. His Word reproduces, and the other nine after its kind follow behind, just like disciples. When you discipline your money, it will have disciples following after it. You discipline your money by tithing.

Until you get to the place where people follow you because of your lifestyle, you're going to have to go get them. It's called evangelism. But when your lifestyle simply draws people, that's evangelism too. No matter how it happens, when people follow after you, that's discipleship; you're reproducing after your kind. Follow me as I follow Jesus. This is important. If you want your money to do this, then you must also do it.

The Tithe looks like *only money*, just as Jesus looked like only a man. Even though the Tithe looks just like the ones it has attracted, it is anointed, commissioned and sent by God's authority. This magnetized $100 bill, the Tithe not only started the whole thing, it powered the entire transaction.

Prove it.

I'd love to.

All we have to do is look at the properties of magnets. If the other $100 bills were also magnets, they may have repelled the Tithe magnet, or attracted other $100 bills to themselves, as magnets do. But they didn't. Since it's the one attracting the nine, we can conclude that it is commissioned, anointed $100 bill magnet that is attracting the other nine, thereby **powering** the deal.

But thou shalt remember the Lord thy God. for it is he that giveth thee the power to get wealth, that he may establish His covenant, which he swear unto thy fathers as it is this day, (Deuteronomy 8:18).

Well, well, well, it takes **power** to get wealth. God gives us **power** when He allows us to use the Tithe. Power is the Tithe because the Tithe is **power money**. God speaks the Word over the Tithe which empowers the Tithe to go out and get wealth. The Tithe is ordained to go out and draw wealth to itself. The more you send out dollar wise, the more wealth you receive back. That is true of the Tithe and of offerings.

It takes **power** to get wealth. Why? Because there are forces that do not want you to get wealth. It's part of our struggle here on Earth.

You may have thought the power you got was the physical strength that you may have received in your body to lift, carry, or tote things and do your job. But have you ever noticed that you make pretty much the same amount of money each week, no matter how tired you are or aren't, as long as your Tithe is consistent? So no matter how much physical power you have or seem to have, you still make the same amount of money.

A spiritual power that God has empowered to work for you is in the Tithe. It's not the physical strength of your body, although you do need that. You need the physical strength. Furthermore, as a Christian, you could have plenty of physical strength, power or energy and not have very much money at all if you are not tithing.

Use of the tithe. And the power of the tithe is one of the awesome ways. God says, *I love you, to us*.

Now we sing *Kumbaya--,* stop by here as that Tithe is traveling at the speed of Godly efficiency. As it comes to you, it brings 9 more just like itself with it. Because you tithe, now you have *increase*. Now you have prospered. Now you have abundance. Your finances, life and godliness have been impacted. Now you have even more faith in God and His Word. Now you are a partaker of the Divine Nature of God. God allows us to participate in the divine when He allows us to do what He does, sow the Tithe. As He sowed Talents to each of us, according to our *several abilities* to start the whole thing off, we receive the increase and **keep** 9X the Tithe when we sow the Tithe back to Him to perpetuate the cycle.

Seed and Increase

For as the rain cometh down, and the snow from heaven, and returneth not thither, but watereth the earth, ad maketh it bring forth and bud that it may give seed to the sower and bread to the eater:

(Isaiah 55:10)

Isaiah 55:9 reads, *His ways are not our ways,* and truly they are not, but we are seeking to be like Him. God promises to give seed to the sower and bread to the eater. That is clearly what He is doing when He provides by the Tithe. It is not the other way around, as we have always thought. We are not providing the Tithe; **the Tithe is *providing* for us.**

Why would God give us a bunch of money and tell us to give 10% of it back to Him, even though it seems to be written that way in the Bible? God is not a man that He should lie. He's not testing us by giving just to take it away, as Job said. If God did give just to take away, why later in the Bible would He say that His gifts are not given unto repentance? (Romans 11:29).

That seeming contradiction is because He's not *giving* you that either. He's allowing you to **use** the Tithe to provide for yourself in the Earth. Just as the breath we breathe is borrowed., so is the Tithe **borrowed**.

To further illustrate this, if you could borrow a tree seed from your neighbor, interest free, that would normally grow one tree, but God anointed the seed for you, and it grew 10 trees--, talk about Divine Nature. You owe the one tree back to the person who lent the seed to you. You would get to keep nine trees for yourself, and not just the usual one tree that an unanointed seed would have produced. As you, seeing how gracious and loving God is to us, are you? That is exactly what he's doing by lending us the Tithe. If you recognize the identity and value of the Tithe, you would be clamoring to be trusted with more Tithe instead of shirking paying what you already owe.

When the trees mature, they will produce another harvest. The harvest produces a harvest. Those nine remaining trees would set you up for certain wealth as they begin to produce a harvest for you for your sowing in the Offering. Each tree can produce 30, 60, or 100-fold of whatever fruit your trees produce, but not until you pay the man back the one tree, the 10th, that you owe him.

Agreement

Why wouldn't God just give us what He wants us to have? This is one of those mysteries that He is revealing. It is not just so we bless it before we send it back to Him, although we do. Maybe that's why we do have to receive it, bless it and send it back, so Heaven and Earth will be in **Agreement**. God created, allows and sends the Tithe because it is crucial to our prosperity. He sends the Word as the Tithe. God would not send the Word if we didn't need the Word; He is not frivolous.

Some say the tithe is to test us. Could be. At first it could be to build character. OK, but why does the cycle not stop? Why would God keep giving you the *same* test over and over? He wouldn't. You must be passing this test, else you wouldn't keep receiving, increase, Tithe, then increase again. Once you pass a test and God sees that you're faithful, honest, not greedy, covetous, or any of the things He's tested you on or trying to teach you, He promotes you. Once you move to the next level, why would He continue to test you? To catch you? Trap you, trip you up? God's not like that. He wouldn't give the same test over and again if you've already passed it.

Do you take a typing test at work every week? Do you take college entrance exams every semester? Do you take a driver's test every day to operate your car? No, no, and no. You may test at first to show aptitude, ability, your *several abilities* and even at intervals to measure progress, but not the <u>same</u> test over and over.

This is a revelation for those who are ready to receive it; others, enjoy your test. It will soon pass, and others will follow, but not the same ones. In God, if you keep getting the same test, it means you're failing. Are all the tithers failing? No, the tithers are passing.

The Tithe is more than a test of obedience or discipline. It is much more. It is a test of **agreement**, authority, and faith. It tests you to see if you're walking in the anointing that you're supposed to be walking in. Do you recognize and acknowledge who you are? And also, can you discern who God is? The answers to all these questions are related to your Tithe. If you answered yes to the above questions, then you probably have no problem paying Tithe. And if you Tithe, then you probably have no problem answering yes and yes to those questions.

When the Tithe goes out and takes on nine more just like itself to create 100% or wholeness, we see a picture of Jehovah Jireh. The Tithe is the seed for he who is to sow again and **nine times the Tithe** is bread for he who will and must eat. This is God's method of replenishing our seed needs and our need for bread. This is God's way of providing us what we need for godliness and our natural life.

As we continue from glory to glory, trying to be like God, we see how He sows, and we do the same. That is why we sow seeds that He graciously provides us. There's power in sowing the Word and seeds.

Recognize that there is a portion of God in every paycheck, in every blessing, and every increase. **10% God and 90% money**. Can you see that? If you can, then you are seeing God.

The Tithe is the Word. There's **power** in the Word and **power** in **Agreement**. When we agree with God, we prosper.

Increase and Seed

Even when asking God for miracle money, God has always sent me what I asked for, plus the Tithe, so, I am able to keep **nine times the Tithe**. For example, once I needed $4568 by Friday, of course. The previous week I had sowed all the money I had, $430. The following Thursday God increased me with a check of $5235. He sent the money that I needed-- $4568, the Tithe of $524 and money leftover--, $143 for an offering and bread to eat. God sent me what I needed and what I asked for, and extra.

Only He didn't really send **extra**, the *extra sent what I needed and asked for*. The **extra** was the **engine** that **powered** the whole transaction, which caused the increase. The **extra** sent the *increase*. The **extra** was the Tithe that sent what I needed, 90%. Since I asked for $4568., God could have sent me that amount. He did, but something had to *cause* $4568 to come to me. You could say that I received manifold return for that $430 offering. OK, that plus. But what *caused* it to come to me? The fact that I sowed? Yes, but it was the Tithe, the extra which was 10% of $5235 or $524 which I sent expediently back to God. There is 10% God in every increase.

God lent me the Tithe on $4568 the previous week to power the deal because he trusted that I'd pay it back. And I recognized it as Tithe. That Tithe went out and collected 9X itself to itself to provide me with *increase*.

Now this is where I insert the reason why you can't participate in offerings. **WITHOUT THE TITHE, NONE OF YOUR MONEY HAS ANY POWER; THE TITHE IS THE POWER**. Notwithstanding the Devourer, If you did have 100-fold increase in a harvest coming to you from a seed you've sown, there's no way it can get to you without the **power money** being in it. **No way.**

As we talk about bread and seed, you can say that the bread is that of which we make sandwiches, and the seed is the brown stuff around those slices of bread. I happen to like the crust, but if I'm supposed to separate it from the bread and send it back to God, I'm going to do it. I won't eat it. I don't need spiritual, and financial indigestion, and neither do you. The crust is what brings us the bread, and even if you cut it off, when you get it, the crust is still what caused you to get the bread, and you get to keep the bread that's on the inside. But you can't get the *inside* of the bread without the ***outside--,*** without the crust.

I used crust as an example because most of the bread is on the inside. You can't get the 90% without the 10%. You can't get the increase without the Tithe, and you won't get the Tithe without the increase because God's Word will always prosper in the thing where He sends it. God graciously allows us to keep most--, 90% of the money. We get to handle the Tithe as long as we are not robbing Him.

To this day, I don't know exactly how that large check came my way or how I received it. I know why. God, and that Tithe I paid, which led to the offering door being opened, in which I sowed a $430 seed. It came from a place that would usually send me a check, but they didn't owe me a check. I called and they assured me that they did. Usually the checks I received from that place were about $2500, or $3000.

I paid the Tithe on the $5235, but that doesn't mean that I now start to receive $5235 per week. *Why not?* Because I didn't have faith for it. **Further, I wasn't even working at the time and did not have a pathway to receive $5235 per week.**

Later, when I was working, I did use my faith to receive as much as I could, to be a faithful servant, all to the glory of God. Amen.

Receiving increase by this principle is not magic. Neither is this a get rich scheme. It is a result of paying the Tithe and sewing in the offering. It is a result of having power money working on your behalf. I repeat, the Tithe is power money. It powers the entire transaction.

How Do I Receive Seed and Increase?

Some experience difficulty receiving increase because they haven't found a *vehicle* or pathway by which *to receive it*. They don't have a job or proper means of **receiving**. Usually that is because of not agreeing with God. If you are tithing and sowing for increase, God has given us all away to receive what He has for us. All of us clamor to receive prosperity through high paying jobs. We all desire to be in a position to receive the most that we can. But even after agreeing with God mentally and understanding and actively tithing, you can disagree by choosing one way for God to bless you while God has chosen another way.

For example, God may have called you to be a pastry chef, but you chose to be a radio DJ. Your average DJ-ing but great at baking. That should be a clue to you, but it's not. You keep trying to get a raise at the radio station and promoted to drive time, unsuccessfully. You're struggling financially, still doing the midnight to 6:00 AM show, and it's been five years. During the day, you're a baking machine, but you give away all your cakes and pies for free. People try to give you money for these yummy baked goods, but you refuse, faking humility. You could really use the money, but you declare, *It's just a hobby*. Would-be customers try to place very large orders for bakery items and wedding cakes, but you tell them you don't have time because of your DJ job, which you are so proud of.

Two of the biggest problems that I've seen in choosing the right career are education and understanding. Many people don't get enough of the right kind of education, and sometimes it's because their understanding is not clear. The title, DJ is more attractive to you and many others than Pie Maker. You may not understand that God has not called you to be a pie maker, but a pastry chef. Being a pastry chef is an awesome job. Further, God calls His people to jobs with dignity. If you knew that, you might be interested in what God says your career should be.

One young man who had the aptitude and opportunity to become an architect didn't, because he really didn't know what an architect was or did. He just thought it was someone who sat at a desk all day and he didn't want to do that. So instead of finding out when the **full** scholarship was offered to him, he *leaned* so far on his then adolescent understanding that he fell over. Now that he's 49, it's too late to use the scholarship; he's a used car salesman.

God's trying to bless you. If you pick one way but He's chosen another, it won't work. **Agree** with God and prosper.

Many choose the lottery, sweepstakes and other seemingly easy ways to receive *increase*. Most of those people are not really tithing for increase anyway. The Tithe is anointed to work; sending plain old *only money*, and not even the right amount to the right place, that is to God at the right time, won't work. The first 10% is the Tithe and it works.

God has placed gifts, skills, talents, and purpose in you. Your parents and teachers have directed you into the path of your life's work, and you should have adhered to instruction. Then you'd be in the right place and position to receive a regular increase. Whatever God intended for you to do to bless you, your increase and prosperity is in that line of work. If you are not prospering at all, it's probably because you need to get a job. If you're employed but prospering very little, struggling or financially frustrated while faithfully observing the spiritual laws of money, you may not be in the right place, position, field, activity, or profession, where God has **commanded** your blessings.

Or maybe you are, maybe you need to renew your mind about who you are, who you are to God, and that you can be blessed. If you don't seem to be getting ahead, don't give up. Spend real time in worship. Remember, after paying the Tithe, offerings are part of your worship. **Agree** with God and prosper.

Recognize the Tithe

When you receive increase, don't get so engrossed while looking at those $100 bills that you forget that God's Tithe is in there. Don't get so selfish, insecure, or rebellious that you disobey God. I don't know why people who are probably broke in the first place want to keep the Tithe. They should be thankful for anything more than what they had. Why be greedy to the point of disobedience? Don't be greedy, put the Tithe back where it goes. Don't allow greed to override gratitude, people. It's gratitude, not greedy, dude.

The Tithe is not trying to stay with you anyway. It's trying to be obedient and get back to God. If you hinder it, God will hinder you. And that's another whole book entitled, **<u>When the Devourer is Rebuked</u>**.

You must recognize the Tithe, though. When the Word of God is disguised as money, it's called the Tithe. That shouldn't deceive you, after you read this book, ever again. That should never be an excuse or stumbling block to you again. If the Tithe is only spiritually discerned and you're having trouble recognizing it, you need to get spiritual.

As said before, the tithe is disguised as money for a reason. When something or someone is wearing a disguise, it's because it has to. It may be in jeopardy, or there's warfare involved. Hello, **financial warfare.**

Jesus wore the disguise of a man, and people, and the devil were still after Him. Jesus and the Tithe are the Word. The Tithe is **disguised** to keep the enemy's hands off of it, not to trick you. If it's a trick, it's not to trick *you* into thinking it's only money, it's to **bypass** the enemy. You're not the enemy, are you? So, you cannot use the excuse that it just looked like money to you, so you spent it. If you're not obedient to tithe, you must discern the tithe. Discernment is usually difficult for non-tithers. Discernment is a gift from God, and he usually doesn't dole out gifts to the disobedient, so you've got to conquer that struggle in your will. Tithe.

The strategy? The Tithe, as the Word is working as it reproduces *after its own kind.* You are an obedient and willing tither who has received the revelation of the **disguise**. The disguise allows the table of Psalm 23 to be set for your prosperity, **even in the presence of your enemies**. This method that God has put in place for you is the way that he feeds you, provides for you, and even blesses you mightily right in the face of those who don't want you to have anything. Right in the midst of enemies who would devour you, God hands you increase and because you tithe. He then says something like this to the Devourer,

Touch not mine anointed, touch neither my child nor his or her increase.

It's like sending supplies in the middle of a war, right under the enemy's nose. Then God takes pleasure in watching you enjoy the fruits of your labor and the prosperity that He provides for you.

The disguise, as it were, is because of financial warfare. It's not to trick you. It's to allow the increase to come to you even in the presence of your enemies. Wake up! There are enemies around you and there are all kinds of battles going on. One of those battles is for your money, or had you not noticed?

Now back to our example. The $1000 in your hand is the Tithe of $100, in this example.

9X the tithe = $1000 (100%), in this example.

You must recognize which portion of the money in your hand is the Tithe and which portion is not. You will also recognize that The tithe is Godly Principal. Working God's principle of tithing is the first instrument of your prosperity. You send the Tithe, the Word immediately on its way back to God. That's the first part. Working the offering for 30, 60 and 100-fold return is another step.

As you put and, keep the Principal in place where it will work for you. And you must also respect the Tithe in the same way. Put it where it belongs, where it will work for you. Where's that? Sown out of your hands, in the church collection basket, and to

God's hand almost anywhere but in your hand at your house or in any bank account with your name on it. Neither should it be in the hands of anyone you know or at the mall.

Well, how do you do that?

By bringing all of the Tithes into the storehouse, (Malachi 3:10).

For example, which 10% of the $1000, *which* $100 do you pay God?

The first one.

You can't give God the wrong $100 even though they are not the same. The way that the Tithe is identified is it is what comes back to God. You identify it as the Tithe, and when He receives it back, God confirms that it's the Tithe. You are agreeing with God, and there's power and Wisdom in agreement. God gave Adam the right to name things. You're naming that $100 as the Tithe.

Only one of the 10 lepers, 10% of them, only one, came back to say thanks and glorify God, (Luke 17:15). The one that came back to say *thank you* was the one that received the anointing to be made whole again, (Luke 17:12-19). The 10th leper received the *anointing* after he came back to say, *Thanks*.

Quoting from my book **Don't Refuse Me, Lord** paying 10% equals saying, *thank you*. With the Tithe, the $100 that comes back to God is the one that received the anointing to be made whole again. That's why you can't pay the wrong $100. The one out of the 10 that comes back to say, *thank you* gets the wholeness anointing. The Tithe is the 10%, that comes back to glorify God. The one that comes back is the Tithe. The money that comes back to God glorifies God and is crowned by Him as the Tithe.

That one, in essence, is recommissioned, re-anointed, empowered, re-appointed, then sent back out to **power** another 9X itself transaction.

The $100 bills that stay with you do not have the *wholeness anointing* until **after** the Tithe is paid. If all the $100 bills stay with you, then none of them will have the wholeness anointing and they don't glorify God. You may use the $900 to glorify yourself with new shoes, new clothes, and a new hat, but God will not be glorified. Further, if you try to keep all ten of the $100 bills, they will all lose their spiritual money magnet properties. The Tithe won't be anointed for 9X increase and you cannot participate in the 30-, 60- and 100-fold offering either. Well, you can *give* in the offering, but it won't be sowing if you are not tithing. As I've said before, you would have no power to receive any increase in the offering if you miraculously had a harvest. It would have no way to get to you. If you don't Tithe, there will be no pathway.

Once the Tithe is paid, the other nine $100 bills receive a *multiplication anointing* if they are sown in the offering and under certain conditions.

Read my book, **The Fold** to uncover why some 30, why some 60, and why some 100-fold return in the Offering.

You can *give* money, but until you pay 10%, the equivalent of the Tithe, you are not sowing for increase. You're simply giving--, how benevolent of you. When you keep the tithe in your purse or wallet, instead of sending it back to God, it becomes *just money* again--, dead presidents on green paper. No anointing--, *just money*. All the money that is with the Tithe, the entire increase is in danger of being lost to you. As I said before, when you spend the Tithe, it's as though the rest of the money becomes *just money* again, then dissolves right before your eyes. Why? Because it can be stolen by the Devourer.

Don't get me wrong, *just money* is good for today. *Just money* is good for just today. But what about tomorrow? What about the future? What about your children's education? What about your children's children? What about those *golden* years?

The Word of God is a highly sophisticated device of **power**, authority, anointing, attraction and purpose, and it works by faith. It is not just letters on a page or words spoken into the air.

To further grasp this, let's imagine you've chartered an airplane that has a ten-person crew on board. The plane and the crew are sent out to pick up 90 passengers, which is the capacity of that particular plane to make a total of 100 people on the plane. The plane lands in the designated city to let all the people off the plane, all 100 of the people who were on the chartered plane are coming to your house. The crew is delivering the people right to your doorstep. The cost to charter was $10,000, but you only had to pay $1000. What a great deal.

Most of the time the crew stays with or near the plane, but even if they made an exception this time and brought the other 90 people right to your living room, you cannot keep the crew or the plane. The crew goes back to the plane to return to the point of origin where they came from. Because the plane and the crew are not yours, it's only chartered for a particular purpose and a set time.

Let's say those 90 people that flew in each bought $100. They're coming to your family reunion at your house. You've been waiting for them. You need them to come to the celebration and they really bless you by coming. You receive the guests and the $9000 that you've been expecting. You had faith that they would get there, and you even sent money toward their arrival. **But you don't keep the plane and the crew just because they bought your loved ones to you**. Neither do you keep the $1000 fee that the airline charged. As a matter of fact, you never were planning to keep the airplane, the crew, or the fee because that would be stealing. It's not your plane, crew or fee.

So why is it when it comes to money that you need, have been expecting and that really blesses you, and that you have paid your 10% to receive, why is it after you receive your 9X, why do you want to keep the plane and the crew that you and God and His Wisdom and Grace and you in agreement with Him, that brought you increase? The Tithe being that $1000 fee. Instead, why not rejoice in the $9000 increase that you get to keep?

Why do people have premeditated stealing on their minds?

It is not *your* Tithe, it's God's. Isn't that double mindedness, having paid the Tithe, having faith that God will bless you, having your hands out to receive increase because of God and planning to steal what is God's at the same time that He is blessing you? Yeah, that's double mindedness and it's treacherous.

Why is it that if we went to the airport to meet the 90 people, you don't covet the plane, crew or the $1000 fee? Is it because you're out in the open, but tithing is on your honor? You shouldn't want to keep the Tithe--, the thing that brought you the increase. Do you respect airport authority more than God? Is it because with God you think you can get away with it? I can't. You can't. We can't. Even if you fold the airplane and the crew up and put them in your pocket and or your purse, you can't steal it and get away with it. Neither can you do that with the Tithe.

Neither can you trick God by leaving the Tithe mixed in with your other money. God is not deceived. He recognizes His Tithe because it's His Word.

The rest of the money is green paper and coins. It is not until after the Tithe is paid that the rest of the money is anointed for 30, 60, or 100-fold return *if* it is sown in the Offering. If it is only a portion of the 90% that is sown, as long as it's sown in faith, God will honor that.

Further, God will **not** rebuke the Devourer for non-tithers. They are powerless against the Devourer. So he has free reign to come in and get whatever was stolen from God. He will come and get whatever you're harboring at your house that belongs to God. You know, the stuff you're acting like and believing is *yours*. That includes the Tithe money itself and whatever you may have bought with the Tithe money as well as anything else he can get his hands on, since he's there. Ultimately, the Devil wants to steal your worship. Whatever you would use for worship to God, that's what he wants.

You don't get to keep the plane, the crew, or the $1000 fee just because it has delivered what it had on board for you.

Consider the bottle that the soda pop comes in. You keep the soft drink and turn the bottle back in for recycling. You let it go. It's got more work to do. It's just as you do with the Tithe after it's done its work on your behalf, you let it go to continue in the way that God has sent it to accomplish. It has to return to God and not return to Him, *void*.

Recommended **When The Devour Is Rebuked** and **Let Me Have A Dollar's Worth**, mini books by this author.

How Does the Tithe Return Void?

The Tithe returns void:

- When it has not prospered.
- When the Tithe has not had the opportunity to multiply.
- If it's been hidden, lost, stolen, or spent, it becomes void.

A check is a promise that money will be paid to you when you present it at the bank. You would void a lost or stolen check, wouldn't you? God voids money that has been stolen or lost to Him as well.

- When the Tithe is not returned to God, by you, God voids the anointing on that money.
- When the devil gets in it.

When the Tithe that was kept gets confiscated by the Devourer because *you* didn't return it, it is voided. It **will** return to God, but its power and value for your sake is cancelled. Even the devil can't hold what is God's so I don't know why you're trying to. The devil couldn't keep Jesus in Hell even though Jesus became sin-laden on our behalf. Though Hell is a sin magnet with lockable gates, the devil cannot contain the Word in it--, tried that already. Jesus is the Word, and the Tithe is the Word. But the Tithe-to-increase-to-Tithe cycle becomes void when the devil gets in it. God can no longer work the godly principle on your behalf if you are not freely returning the Tithe back to Him. When the Tithe gets into the enemy's hand, it is not reactivated to become whole again, because if it were, the one who sent it back to God would receive increase. And God ain't prospering the devil, so He voids the anointing on that particular Tithe, so you lose three times.

- Once by having what you used the Tithe for stolen from you by the Devourer.
- Twice, as the anointing on the Tithe is now inactivated on your behalf by God, and.
- A third time because the money, the 90% that you could use for an offering for 30-, 60-, and 100-fold return is also not anointed for that.

Instead, its attractiveness to 30-, 60-, or 100-fold itself *after its kind* is cancelled. Until you work the Tithe, the other money you have won't work in the offering. Next week's blessing is at risk, but you won't realize that until later, when lack, insufficiency, or unforeseen expenses hit you.

If repentance and changes are not made immediately, the day you steal the Tithe is the day the downward spiral begins, financially and otherwise. To summarize, you lose by what you stole gets stolen from you. What criminal can report such a crime and to what authority? And you lose some time, some way, something in the future because of the Devourer--, time and thing to be announced. Neither you nor I know what it is until it happens.

If you really want to see Jehovah Jireh in His Glory, tithe. If you desire to see El Shaddai in action sow in the offering for up to 100-fold increase.

Prosper in your soul regarding releasing the Tithe. Release worry and fear about not having enough. God will make sure you have no trouble living on 9X what you tithe.

If you desire more money, ask yourself if God can trust you with a larger plane and crew? Can you manage a larger vehicle and crew? Do you have enough money and discipline to charter a larger plane and crew?

When the crew is larger it will still go out and attract 9X itself. The size of the Tithe determines the size of the crew and the plane that does the work of collecting increase for you. A crew of 20 will bring in 180 people. A crew of 100 people with a larger plane (greater faith), can bring 900 people and so on. But if you still have the 100-passenger plane and you're tithing for more than a 100 person increase, the Word says you won't have room to receive it and you won't receive it unless you make room to receive. If you send out a larger crew (more Tithe) you will need to provide a greater vehicle (means or pathway for God to bless you). You need a bigger plane. Ask God to help you move to a position or job where you can receive the increase and keep 9X the Tithe that you pay. The better paying job is your vehicle.

And stated earlier, if you don't pay Tithes then eventually God will move you to a job that pays 9X what you tithe. No job--, no Tithe equals no job.

God can bless you anywhere and in any way He chooses, but the most expedient way is when you have your own business. No, I did not say quit your job and start your own business. Ask God. Also, I recommend that you read my book **Don't Work for Money** to get a picture of how God can move for the self-employed.

Don't get a larger crew (Tithe) if you don't have a larger plane (faith) to receive more. Pay what you owe, but do not pay more Tithes than you have Word and faith for. You may choose to start out small and build your faith. Don't get so excited about this principle that you misuse this application. If you do, you may risk disappointment in God. But if you work this and any other principles of God correctly, you will be rewarded accordingly. It doesn't matter how much you tithe or how much your Tithe is, as long as you're faithful with your 10%, because it will still get you into the 30, 60, and 100-fold offerings.

The amount that you're entrusted with to tithe sets the stage for how much you have left over; you'll have 9X more to sow Offering. Therefore, you want to be very faithful with the Tithe so that you will be entrusted with more and more Tithe as well as more and more 9X so you can have more to sow in the Offering.

What is the Word?

When I say the Tithe is the Word I don't literally mean Jesus Christ. The Bible says that Jesus was given as an offering. What I mean is that the Word spoken out of the mouth of God that goes forth (Isaiah 55:9-11) to perform a task and then returns to the one who sent it. What it does and how it performs is by God's Word and for the purposes of our study, it's called, *Tithe*.

What is the Word that God uses to cause increase to come your way? Is it tithe or abundance? Or is it the word prosperity spoken as its assignment? It could be wholeness; whatever God has named it or names it. In your particular case it works. You call it the tithe when you pay it, and when God receives it, he will signify it as the tithe and Commission it for wholeness by using whatever word he uses to cause it to go out and get nine times itself. That has already spoken this word and even confirms it by saying that as long as the earth remains, there will be seed time and harvest. This is his way of telling us that the principle of tithing that allows you to keep nine times what you tithe and opens the door for offerings is in effect.

The Lord will come... Behold, his reward is with him, and his work before him, (Isaiah 40:10).

The Lord comes and. His reward is with Him., The Word has the Tithe, it has collected *after its kind.* The Tithe comes and its reward is with it. The reward is 9X and it's for you because you Tithe.

And his work is before Him--, the Tithe. As we present the Tithe back to God, we honor Him, acknowledging Him as the one who caused this Word and principle to work on our behalf. He is the one who has prospered us. He is the one who has caused this Word, disguised as money, to multiply after its kind and present to us 9X what we tithe, on which we can live and thrive. God's Word performs and **waters** the Earth--, we too, are the Earth, (Isaiah 55).

Do you believe the Word?

Do you believe the Word you say? You do. But faith without works is dead. So, if you want to have some works that prove you believe the Word, participate in tithing. The Tithe is the Word. If you believe the Word, do the Word--, Tithe.

You Can't Keep the Tithe at Your House

You can't keep the tithe if you want to prosper, because in the economy of God, the Tithe is the principle thing in your earning a living. It's the principal thing, in your receiving things that pertain to life and godliness. It's the Principal because it draws money and prosperity to itself. It's God's Principal. And because it's God's and anointed, it's packed with power.

God has spoken the Word over that 10%. You can't keep it. It's God's. It's the Word and it's God's. It's to do his work, then it's on it's way back to Him.

The Devourer is waiting to consume the Tithe, the accursed thing, unless and only unless it is where he can't get to it, and the only place that the Devourer can't get to it is:

- When it's working, attracting 9 more like itself to itself. The devil never succeeded at intercepting Jesus, the Word, and he can't intercept the Tithe when it's working, so you

must always keep the Tithe working, not laying around your house.
- When is delivering 9X to you. Nothing can separate you from the love of God which is in Christ Jesus. The devil cannot separate you from the Word or the Word from you unless you let him. The Devourer cannot take the Tithe from you if you're working it.
- When it's on its way back to God. As stated before, the devil could not hold Jesus even on his own turf. Even in Hell with a home field advantage, the devil still lost. Jesus kicked the devil's behind even at an away game in Hell.

You cannot keep the Tithe for at least three reasons.

1. It's not keepable. Why? Because it's **God's**, and it is the Word of God. As the Word of God, it **must** return to God. There's no way you can contain it, hold it, or restrain it. Neither can you protect it from the Devourer.
2. You can't keep it because it's keeping you. It's keeping you in prosperity, providing the things for your life and godliness. You cannot stop the Word of God because it obeys **God**. Remember, as we established, the Tithe is the Word.
3. You can't keep the Word of God because it's greater than you are. You can't keep anything that's greater than

you are. The devil found out that Jesus is greater than he is when trying to keep Jesus in Hell.

You, by disobedience, can cut off the anointing of your Tithe to work for you, but as the Word, it can be reactivated, or re anointed by God and agreement to work in the Earth for whomever has it, and whoever has faith to use it and is faithful to receive it, pay it, returning it to God. Just as God gave **all** to the faithful servant in the parable, where did he get it?

From the unfaithful or wicked servant.

Pay close attention to this. Because of general disobedience with the Tithe, there are fields and fields of Tithes out there for the picking, as God is taking away all from the unfaithful wicked servants who don't tithe, don't give offerings, and don't multiply the money they're entrusted with. All you have to do is show yourself faithful in what God has given you so far. Then the millions of men who have lost their Talents, their tithes, will be sorrowful as it is taken away from them. It will be given to those of us who are faithful. And the faithful will rejoice when given more Tithes, which when paid, will go out, multiply after its kind, and bring increase and activate the 90% to 30, 60 and 100- fold return when sown in the offering. This is God's plan.

But the average man's plan is to not tithe.

No Tithe equals no 9X the Tithe.

No Tithe equals no increase.

No Tithe equals, no Devourer rebuked.

No Tithe equals no windows opened.

No Tithe equals no poured out blessings.

No Tithe equals no preservation of fruit on the vine.

No Tithe equals, no offerings.

No Tithe equals no 30-fold, no 60-fold, no 100-fold returns. Ultimately, no prosperity, no wealth.

Because of robbing God in dealing falsely with money, the Curse of the Law must and will come (Deuteronomy 28), even on those who are saved. I understand that unsaved folk don't tithe, but for anyone who professes Christ, except for the Mercy of God, there is no escape.

As believers, our escape from the Curse of the Law, (Galatians 3:13), is genuine repentance and obedience to this principle.

Tithe.

A Well-Tuned Instrument

The Tithe is God's instrument for your prosperity. *That* He allows you to use it is reason for praise.

While writing this book, the Holy Spirit kept showing me a boomerang. God sends His Word out like a well-tuned instrument that knows how far to go, what path to take and how and when to turn around and come back to the sender. A boomerang is one such instrument. Since it is also a weapon used for hunting, once it is in motion, it is very dangerous. If you interfere with it while it's working, it could hurt or even kill. Many who interfere with the Tithe also find that messing with it backfires on them.

The Tithe also boomerangs, but in a good way, it comes back to the sender, God, to be sent out again.

Increase will travel in your path. It will come to you if you have been obedient and faithful with your tithes. But if you haven't tithed, sorry for you, increase goes to the tither. Prosperity is God's plan for His people. Seedtime and Harvest is still in effect. Although paying the Tithe gets you into the Offering, tithing has its own set of perks and associated increases and blessings. The Tithe is out collecting, attracting, and reproducing *after its kind,* 9X itself and opening Offering doors for you. Are you receiving any of it? Are you entering into the 30-, 60- and 100-fold offering?

Legalistically, if you earn $1000, your required Tithe payment is $100, but it is your minimum. Recall, the Principal should be as much as possible. Godly Principal, which is the Tithe in this book, should also be as much as possible. I'm not telling you to put your whole paycheck in the collection plate, unless you're paying first fruits. But, put as much as possible, as much as you have a Word on, and faith for, on which to receive increase. Don't tithe anymore over the required 10% then you have faith for, but tithe. Don't sow offerings any greater than what you have faith for, but sow in the Offering.

If you are a tither, as that boomerang that God has sent out comes to you, having reproduced after its own kind, having nine more like it with it, you'll keep what is on board for you, but you won't try to keep the boomerang, that is the Tithe, itself.

Use Wisdom. How do you expect to catch a boomerang that you didn't throw? And if you do, how do you expect to *keep* it? And if you did, what are you going to do with it? Are you planning to send the Word out yourself? *Where and to what end?* It's not your Word, it's God's. We acknowledge that we can't anoint it. We don't really know what the Word that God speaks over it; God has to send it out, to start the whole process. What do you plan or think you could accomplish by sending out the *boomerang*? Even in the natural you just get a boomerang back, if you know how to throw one. If you don't know how to throw a boomerang but you throw a boomerang, you won't get anything back. Because without anointing, it's just a boomerang, A child's toy.

If you don't know how to throw that boomerang, you may never see it again. And that's like the Tithe. When you send God's Tithe out to good causes and needy friends, it doesn't multiply on the way *to* them. But it makes you feel good and eases your conscience. It makes you look like a hero.

Because the money you send out doesn't multiply on its way *to* friends and loved ones, that proves you don't know what to say over it. This boils down to not knowing how to throw our hypothetical boomerang. If you lend them $50 when they get it, it's still $50. When (if) you get it back from them, it's still only $50. So, neither you nor they know what to say over money, either. They cannot anoint or commission it for wholeness, only God.

Personal debtors may pay you back with interest and may even double it or pay you $100 for the $50 loan, like so many loan sharks--, but not 9X. Without God's anointing, it cannot multiply. It comes and goes as *just money* to your friends, and you've just lost the Tithe, the anointing on the Tithe, by putting it in the hands of anyone *other than* God or His representatives in the Earth--, even for a moment.

Your friends also cannot protect the Tithe--, yours or theirs from the Devourer. If you told me I have $100, it's my Tithe, but you can borrow it until Sunday, I wouldn't want it. No one should. It's accursed. Accursed means set aside for God's use. When you give the Tithe to places and people other than God, He **voids** the power on that money, or your disobedience does it automatically. Usually, you never see it again anyway. When you withhold the Tithe for whatever reason--, you're mad at the pastor, or baby needs a new pair of shoes, you risk not only losing the Tithe but everything else because that unleashes the Devourer.

You should not want to keep the Tithe because the Tithe is the Principal. The Tithe is the goose that's laying the golden eggs. The Tithe is the Word of God, and it must go back to Him. The Tithe is God's and it's from God, the hand that's feeding you. Keeping the Tithe is stealing from the person who blessed you is the same as biting the hand of our provider, Jehovah Jireh. God is your Source, not your boss, employer, Mama, or daddy. God is your source.

Have you ever read a soft drink bottle that says 10% juice? Similarly, **there's 10% God in every dollar and in every paycheck**, and in every increase there's a Tithe. There's a Tithe in every dollar you get. The Tithe is the *juice*, the **extra**, the power. And it's in every increase you receive. All money comes to you with the Tithe already in it, all money comes to you because the Tithe is in it. Learning to work that system of tithing is a must before you can get into the **Offering**. It is the same as learning how to bank and earn in the good old days 10% before you begin investing in the stock market. Participating in the offerings for 30-,60-, and 100-fold return to earn even higher returns.

The Tithe is the principle that's making the money for you. **You are not making the money for yourself, and you are not making the money for God.** You're at your job, it's true, but you are in the economy of God. You should be witnessing to folk and representing God as you do your work so you can receive your wages. Receiving your wages and much more will be so much easier and assured if you tithe, and those promises God says we will reap, we will reap with joy and enjoy the fruits of our labor, (Ecclesiastes 2:24).

Nine Times the Tithe

> And to one he gave 5 talents, and to another two and to another, one. To every man according to his *several abilities,* and straightway took his journey.
> (Matthew, 25:15).

One of the high paying jobs in the Kingdom of God while still on Earth is Tithe handling. Considering that we get paid in spiritual money for a lot of ministry, we need to allow God to bless us anyway He chooses. This particular pay is 9 X itself. That is, whatever you tithe, you get to keep 9X that amount for yourself, and God will always make sure you have no trouble living on 9X what you tithe. I don't know another line of work that pays that kind of return or gives such commissions or bonuses. God allows you to keep the 90%, only having to pay 10%. God does not even ask for 50%. He doesn't even match it, saying what you tithe, you can keep the exact same amount for yourself. He gives you 9X what you tithe to keep for yourself on which to live. Of course, you want use some of it to finance your godliness as well, which is offerings and charity.

The remarkable thing is. That you're not even paying any of *your* money and that it's all **God's** money. It's just though He makes us an interest free loan that is designed to make money for us so we can have money and He lets us use it to be blessed. He keeps on blessing us.

Being selected as a Tithe handler is related to your desire to handle it. And we all have or should have a desire to have and handle money. Tithe handling is commensurate with your obedience, diligence, and timeliness and sowing it back to God, which also shows desire. The amount you start with is related to your *several abilities*. That's why you need to be building yourself up in the Word of God, the things of God, and coveting the best gifts so you will have a lot of abilities.

Also, these things may come into play.

- Your past history of managing God's money or repentance if you don't have a good spiritual financial resume.
- Obedience and willingness in doing it.
- Faith and faithfulness.
- The type of vehicle you have for receiving increase.

But it's not all about the *vehicle*. I know plenty of doctors, lawyers and other professionals who have great *vehicles*. Not their automobiles, but a great capacity for receiving increase, but are not wealthy or well-off people. There are a lot of criteria for being financially blessed. It is not all about positioning yourself in a job that traditionally pays well. Conversely, many people have many small legal businesses that make them a bundle.

Expert Tithe handlers often have the spiritual gifts of giving, faith, and administration, among others. They are unselfish, organized, and move in love. They are praisers. If you don't have or don't think you have the best gifts, God will bring you discipline by the process of tithing and these gifts will develop in you. It's one of the ways you cultivate some of the Fruit of the Spirit, such as faithfulness and patience.

There are many levels of promotions in this job. You get promotions and the job of Tithe handling by being all of the above and:

- Increasing your faith with corresponding action.
- Acknowledging God in all things so He can help you increase your ability to receive. God will allow you to handle more and more, making you a channel of blessings.

Remember.
- The Tithe does not like to be delayed on its way back to God.
- The Tithe does not like to be coveted by humans and other little g *gods*.
- The Tithe is not likely to be left lying around.

- The Tithe is accursed and therefore set aside for God's use, not for *your* use. You keep 90% of your increase for your use.
- The Tithe does not like being in precarious situations or subjected to the Devourer.

Once the Tithe is gone out and collected 9X itself to itself is still not accomplished all it set out to accomplish. It has not completed its assignment until it drops off 9X s to the tither, that is, *waters the Earth,* and returns to God. Being set aside for God's use, God will probably send it out to do that same job again on your behalf, but it has to be returned to God and be re-anointed after each transaction of Tithe-to-increase cycle.

The Tithe returns to God to report.

- It states it's done its job.
- Its arrival speaks of your faithfulness, that you are indeed the one who sent it back to God.
- The Tithe's, arrival, reports of your timeliness in paying it back to God.
- When the Tithe gets there, God checks to see if it is indeed the Word or the Tithe, not a counterfeit or something *like* a Tithe.
- And it confirms that it is just. That when God puts His stamp of approval on it.
- Agreement is reached and agreeing with God is always profitable and wise.

Other Tithers are receiving the same blessings as you, commensurate with their Tithes, their capacity to receive, and their faith in God--, their *several abilities.*

Tithing is God's principle that is allowing very high dividends of 9X what you Tithe to be deposited back into your hands. And the Tithe is the Principal that you pay, offering is what you sow; both are as investing. Principal in the natural is used to make you money, but you don't spend the Principal, even though you know it's yours. When you get the Tithe in with the increase, you don't keep or spend the Tithe. Just as Principal is making you money, you know it's yours. You don't keep or spend the Principal, you keep working it. So in reaping, in Seedtime and Harvest, the Tithe is reproducing *after its kind,* in the Divine Nature of God,

What If You Have Become Powerless?

If you're suffering financial impotence, then you have lost the Tithe. You don't have any Principal, Godly or otherwise.

But as one was felling a beam, the axe head fell into the water, and he cried and said, alas, master, for it was borrowed, (2 Kings 6:5)

The axe head was borrowed. At least the man who unfortunately lost the axe head was *working* with it. It wasn't just lying around while he decided if he was going to steal it like so many do with God's Tithe, the Tithe is also borrowed. Most who have lost their Tithe weren't even working it. They had stolen or were in the process of stealing it when they lost it, that's *how* they lost it.

If you have lost your Tithe, there can still be a powerful instrument in the hands of whomever God gives it to. Even if you've lost it, or if it's taken from you, it can still be an instrument of power. You just don't have it anymore. You've in essence become powerless. But the Tithe that is lost to you is of great value to anyone who receives it, recognizes it and knows how to work it.

And the Tithe is still God's --,talk about taking care of what is another man's.

Jesus did not stop being Jesus even at the Cross. Even in Hell, He was still the Son of God on loan to Earth for a purpose set forth by God. Even in Hell, he was still the Word. The Word is still the Word; always & forever--, that doesn't change when you've lost the Tithe. You've misplaced, lost or misused something of great value. Like the man with the lost axe head. You should be distressed and take immediate action.

Imagine losing a 50-carat diamond. Don't you think someone will pick it up? It's still a diamond. Just because you lost it doesn't change its value, just your net worth. Some of the signs you've lost your Tithe are.

- You're broke. Your net worth is decreased or diminished completely.
- You regularly run out of money too soon.
- You're bombarded with unexpected expenditures often. The Devourer is on the loose at your house or in your life.
- Your life is compromised because of money.

You don't have to throw your hands up and wonder what happened. I'll tell you. You lost your

Tithe. You lost it by disobedience, ignorance or rebellion. Even if you've lost your Tithe, that's still very valuable. Someone else can pick it up. How? Well like the wicked servant from the parable lost his ONE Talent. When the Tithe is not treated the way God says to handle it, no matter what hell it goes through, ultimately it is returned to God, and becomes laid up. Wicked servants of parable fame did nothing with the Tithe, thereby laying it up. Misplaced a\or hidden Tithes are in houses, wallets, purses, shoe boxes, mattresses, malls, in some backyards, anywhere but tithing envelopes. Hidden Talents--, monies do not please God. He gives much grace and many opportunities to correct the behavior. If you've ever lost a job or lost out financially, it's because your tithe wasn't working for you. God takes Tithes from those who aren't paying or working the tithe Because. It's his and gives it to faithful servants.

You might be looking at your neighbor. Or a co-worker thinking he's not as educated as I am or he's *dumber* than I am. Why does he have more success? **Perhaps he's tithing.**

The Tithe has power. God allows use of for prosperity, but in measure until He can trust us with more. Work it, work it. Make it work for you. Seriously, look at your life, financial and otherwise, is the power of God working in your life? Tell yourself the truth. What is the power of God doing for you? You should be secure of all promises of God, even in the midst of enemies, (Psalm 23:5). If not, the power of God is not working fully in your life.

Those who are not making full use of the power of God are struggling, frustrated, tired and worn out. They are using energy in the natural that could be used in the spiritual to affect much greater things. If God put you here to be a Bible teacher, for example, but you never do it because of being consumed with money and money worries, even if you have great success with money, you have not done the greater thing, as God designed your money to work by 9X the Tithe, then then 30-, 60-, and 100-fold in the offering.

But you're only earning 10% in your mutual fund. You're not doing the greater thing.

At least if you put your money to the lenders, as He said in the Parable of the Talents, you could earn some interest on it. But that's still not the greatest thing. Your money should work hard for you, so you don't have to work so hard. Doing the greater thing is much easier than not if you're not availing your money to God's system of increase. No wonder you don't have as much as you could or should. God is not just interested in us; He dotes on us. We see El Shaddai, the God of more than enough in His glory.

If you've lost your Tithe all the money you currently have, if you have any money you've lost, you've got the weakest, most ineffective money. It's the worst thing that can happen to you. If you choose to spend, misuse or give away the Tithe, that was the worst decision you could have made. It is worse than losing the Principal because there are not as great spiritual consequences for losing Principal in the natural, as for losing God's Tithe. Losing Principal is unfortunate, but there are not as many spiritual ramifications compared to losing the Tithe.

As a Christian, you've got to answer to God, as did the three with the Talents. If you are judged unfaithful, permission to enter into the joy of the Lord will not be granted. Losing the tithe, the axe head --, is losing the most important part. It's the part that does the work. Of all the money you could have lost, you've lost the power. You'd better call for the man of God, preacher, prophet, pastor, somebody. First repent asking God to forgive you, then ask Him to restore the Tithe to you. Ask Him to give you another chance, another opportunity to work with the Tithe, to be a Tithe handler. To be again trusted to do what is right concerning money.

If you've lost the Tithe, run to God, not away from him. Do it right now.

Being In the Right Place at the Right Time

The Tithe is the Word of God disguised as money, just as Jesus was the Word of God disguised as a man. When the Word of God is clothed in flesh, it's called Jesus. When the Word is cloaked as money, it's called the Tithe.

God's Word is going back and forth in the Earth, descending from the mouth of God to the ears and hearts of man, as well as to the hands and all things that obey the Word of God. It is also ascending back to God as we pay the Tithe in agreement with God. As the world is traveling at the speed of Godly efficiency, reproducing after its own kind, all we have to do is be in the right place at the right time.

Where is that? Where is that right place?

No worries, if it's the Tithe, it will find you. If it's any other blessing, it's going usually to the one who asked for it by sowing for it in faith. Or it's going where God pleases, where God has commanded the blessing, wherever God tells you to be, and wherever God's Word is going forth. Wherever God's Word is working, be there. And because of the nature of God and the great abundance that His Word is effecting and working in the Earth. We can also receive in the overflow.

Receive what?

Whatever we have faith to receive.

What does God want Out of the deal?

He wants His people to prosper, and He wants His Word back. He will graciously allow us to use the tithe and keep 9X what we Tithe for life and godliness.

God's Word equals prosperity. It prospers in the thing that pleases Him, and it prospers in the thing that he sends it forth to accomplish. Prosperity means living in abundance. My definition of abundance is *a whole lot of.*

He sent His Word and healed them (Psalm 107:20). As it pertains to healing, for example, God's Word sometimes masquerades as medicine. Sometimes it's masked as exercise. Go and show yourself to the priest, (Matthew 8:4). Going to the priest took faith, but it also was exercise. Lepers weren't even allowed in the gates of the city. They were as far as possible from the temple, so getting to the priest was a good little trek. God sends water. Healthy foods and lifestyles, and sometimes medical procedures offer healing. In the Bible, God's Word was sometimes spit in clay. God's Word can be wrapped up in the hands of a capable surgeon or diligent pharmacist. Sometimes God's Word is a spoken word. **Lazarus come forth.**

Many times, God's Word has been the essence of mom's, chicken soup or a kiss to make it all better. God's Word has shown up as a man, Jesus the Christ, and His Word comes to us regularly for our finances masked as money, called the Tithe.

God's Word may come disguised or hidden, but it is unveiled and manifesting in renewed spirits, increased finances, healed bodies, and prospered souls.

Wherever the Word is going back and forth, be in the midst of it, and you can receive in the abundance of overflow more than you could ever think or ask. This does not mean if you're saved to not tithe or only stand around and glean from others who are sowing. It means pay attention. Because of where you are sometimes your blessing may be discreet or may need to be discerned. God's not trying to trick you, He's trying to get your blessing to you through a financial War Zone in the presence of your enemies.

Until you and God clear the air spiritually and completely, all of Earth is a financial war zone. God is working to get your blessing past your enemy to you.

Your increase may first show up as an increase in your Tithe.

In money, God gives 9X the Tithe. Every aspect of God's economy boasts abundance as the man or woman of God is praying for a certain something, say healing--, you who are seated in the audience may get healed too. What if God sent 9X the healing with every Word for healing? What if He sends 9X this, 9X that, 9X everything or more knowing God? I don't believe He sends to waste, but I believe that God sends to abundance. If you are a tither, He just might. That hasn't been revealed to me yet.

Kings and royalty move in great abundance. Recall that the Queen of Sheba traveled with her great retinue, and she was an earthly queen. How much more is our God with what a great retinue is the King of kings traveling? When God said, **Let there be light,** He may have looked in his caravans to see what kind of light was there. There was an abundance of it, not just a candle or a 40-watt light bulb. God filled the Earth with light three days before he created the sun and the moon.

So, when God spoke healing to the assembly where you were, there was a power of healing in the air, a permeation and abundance of it. In this great abundance you may get healed in the overflow. That type of manifestation is usually dramatic and obvious.

Or the minister may be praying for finances for the congregation, and you get blessed too. Your finances get jolted, lifted, enhanced, knocked up a few notches. Hallelujah. But you may not recognize it because it's usually not dramatic and obvious. Money is not falling from the sky. Well, it is falling from the balcony in some services, I hear, but not from the sky that I know of. God sends His Word to bless you. Your blessing is **disguised** as *only money*. But now you know what to do.

Don't ignore it and miss your blessing and stay where you are financially. How do you recognize it? By the Spirit and by obedience, God may whisper in your heart, Start paying blank dollars more in with your Tithe. Or the prophet may say it to you, audibly. That's how God is trying to get more increase to you. So do it. You may not have the 30-, 60-, or 100-fold yet faith yet, but the means to receive that kind of increase right now. But you do have 9X faith. Go ahead, do it. You may just need that increase in power to receive this substantial blessing that is God's next increase for you.

Not recognizing the Tithe and investing in it as Godly Principal, you spend it. Unfortunately, by spending the Tithe you call it something other than what God has named it. Again, proving that you don't know what to call it. You can't rename the Word after God has named it. Talk about disagreeing with God. You can't call the Tithe *just money* after God has called it the Tithe, and then take it to the mall; that nullifies and voids the whole blessing. The mall can't multiply your money 9X. It can't multiply it at all; only God can do that. By recognizing the Tithe and investing in it as the Tithe, putting it in its proper place, the church offering basket. Even as that powerful Word is moving and spoken over you, don't miss it.

These opportunities for increase do not just happen in a church service. God can speak to you anytime, in any way He chooses, even through a book. Selah.

If someone blessed you with unpopped corn, would you know what it was? Would you recognize it as a blessing? Would you recognize unpopped popcorn? Most people would. Would you eat unpopped corn? No. You'd wait for the process and the popping to get the most out of the corn and not break your teeth. This is such a simple test of faith, patience, and mostly discipline. Yet while it is unpopped, it is still a blessing to receive. All you have to do is pop it. Only a child would frown on or refuse unpopped popcorn, usually because of not knowing what it is or what to do with it, or they don't have the patience to wait for it to become popped. A spiritually immature person may be the same way about the Tithe. *It's already money,* they may rationalize. *Why do I have to **give** it to make it more money? Why do I have to wait? Why do I have to wait by faith, not being able to see what's happening to this money while it multiplies? Can I just use this?* Those are the questions of a child.

Sowing, paying the Tithe, brings a greater blessing. When you receive the instruction to Tithe for greater and sustained increase from God or the man of God, you will obey by faith and realize that blessing. You will gain patience because faith builds discipline and patience.

The Tithe also needs to be exposed to a process to get the most out of it. Think of the Tithe as unpopped prosperity, and you know a handful of popping corn can yield a great bowl full of bounty. The same is true for the Tithe. And you know how to add water to the condensed soup or the concentrated fruit juice, right? Or do you just eat or drink it straight from the can?

By faith, the Tithe is concentrated cash, frozen finances, unpopped, prosperity. It must be exposed to, whatever the process or the elements, the offering basket, prayers of agreement, God's anointing, whatever is God's process to become full, whole and complete.

In the case of the Tithe, in the case of God's multiplication is also exposed to its own kind, so it can attract and collect more like itself to itself. It wants to grow, expand, and prosper. You submit it to the process of becoming what it is.

In the case of the Tithe, that process is: Take it to church. Signify it as the Tithe, thereby agreeing with God. Bring all the Tithes into the storehouse, (Malachi 3:10). Consecrate the Tithe back to God, (Micah 4:13).

Now that you are an obedient and faithful tither, God looks on your several abilities to see if He can increase your Tithe. That's His plan to prosper you. Do you recognize it?

Like so many complaining employees whose responsibility gets increased before their pay, your employer is grooming you for a new position as it gives you more responsibility even though the pay may not reflect the new position yet. God is grooming you for a new position and increased prosperity in the Kingdom when He increases your Tithe. It may not look like it, but we walk by faith, not by sight. An increase in Tide means a raise in pay is on the way. By faith. It's only a matter of time.

Some of you reading this book are about to get a raise and promotion. You may feel it's a demotion when you first obey God because you may have less tangible money than your used to having, but by faith you have more because God just increased your Tithe, He's told you to start paying more Tithe. He's grooming you for your new position in Him. Until you are discerning or the money manifests you may not feel as though an increase in the Tithe, is a promotion .Just as when you are being groomed for a promotion at work, without faith, until the money shows up in your paycheck, you may not fully grasp the reality of promotion or recognize it as a blessing.

When you hear this Word, quickly agree with God, and since you're one of the just, you're walking by faith.   Freely you have received, so freely give, (Matthew 10:8). If God gives you 9X what you Tithe, then 30-, 60, and 100-fold in the offering. Whatever else you have asked God for, chances are you got *more* than you needed when you got yours. Be in the right place wherever the Word of God is going forth. There's abundance and overflow. Now that you've received abundantly, find someone who has had the same need used to have and minister to them.

Your Financial Portfolio

By all means, with Wisdom, put your money into any investments that you choose, but don't rely solely on the world's system failing to invest in God's way. God's system is what supports the world's system anyway, and it's what they copied, *sort of.* The world's principle is the copy of God's Tithe--, *sort of.* God's Tithe attracts *after its kind*, and so does the world's principle--, *sort of.*

Why, sort of?

God's Tithe attracts 9X more like itself to itself and flows to you. The world's principal attracts an average interest of about 0.09X itself, which is 9% on a good day. When what is *after its kind* comes into your account, the bank or the financial institution charges to manage and disperse it to you, God doesn't levy any additional fees.

Covet the best gifts; ask God for your measure of Talents based on your *several abilities*. Invest the Talents wisely and become a Tithe handler. The pay is 9X the Tithe. If you're already a faithful, cheerful, tither, praise God.

God said that He would give us the things that pertain to life and godliness, but he didn't say He'd give it all at once. That's the mistake many get-rich-quick people make. Think about this: **God may actually give you the equivalent of 10 talents of silver or gold to sow as your Tithe over your entire lifetime.** What have you done with the allotment you've received so far? What *will* you do with the rest of your Talents?

A lifetime of Biblical Talents will be about $20,000 to $40,000 if in silver and $300,000 to $600,000 if in gold. That is, if you sow your Talents, you would earn between $200,000 to $600 million in your lifetime just by tithing. We haven't even talked about entering to increase from offerings yet. The average adult who earns $40,000 per year may work for 25 years to earn about $1,000,000. See how God's investment of 10 talents based on your *several abilities* is contributing to what would be sizable increase for your life and godliness?

Always be alert for sustained increase as well as one time and intermittent rewards. God gives miracle money. Remember, sustained increase may come as an increase in the Tithe amount first. The other blessings rewards gifts. Some miracle money generally flow after the offering as God may be giving you the good and faithful servants that *front money*, Talents, Godly principle, or Tithe, which used to belong to the unfaithful servant. See it as a reward, not a burden state. Cheerful when God tells you to increase the Tithe, or offering, for that matter.

10 Times the Tithe

For clarity's sake, I must explain that we appear to receive increase of 10 X the Tithe. So if a Tithe of $50 per week brings a paycheck on Friday at $500?, the paycheck is 10 times the Tithe. Ten times 50 is 500, but that's assuming the whole cycle started from nothing. If we assume it started from nothing, then we are not acknowledging God. Instead, we give ourselves credit for having $500 on Friday and through faulty thinking we risk not paying God what belongs to Him.

But it started from something--, seed, front money, 10 Talents, faith, along with an anointed Word from God, who says to the Tithe, go and draw 9X to yourself, and bring it to my faithful servant. Or whatever the spoken Word or assignment is. Remember, we get to keep 9X the Tithe, not 10X the Tithe. There's more. God continues speaking to His Tithe, **Then return to Me.**

When the Tithe I pay comes back to me with 9X itself on board for me, that identifies me as a faithful servant, and I like that.

The transaction started with 10 Talents, or the 10% which **belongs to God**. Remember, there is a Tithe in every increase. That's how the increase got to you. We've described it as **extra**. As a plane and a crew as a boomerang, as the engine, and as the Word of God. Every increase is powered by its internal engine (anointing, power). The Tithe, the paycheck of $500. So simple math shows us that 10% of $500 is $50.

When you think of your $500 paycheck is because of you, you will not acknowledge God. Not considering God in your financial transactions is exactly why you are tempted to not tithe. When you don't consider God on Sunday, by Friday you'll about swear you caused your own increase. Never swear.

Honoring God on Sunday, the first day of the week keeps him on your mind all week as you see the temptation to steal the Tithe comes long before the money gets in your hand. Because of that temptation, we need to plan to pay the Tithe and plan not to keep it. Don't wait until you get to church on to see how you feel if the choir sings your favorite song. Or if the preacher's sermon doesn't offend you, no conditions. Tithe paying is not based on your conditions, but on God's it's based on the Word and law of God, and those are His conditions.

The enemy may create financial needs to fuel your temptation to steal the Tithe, by broken cars, flat tires, old shoes, and clothes. You may be thinking how much more you need this money. You're thinking that this money can solve those problems. Oh yeah, temporarily. But the problems that come from stealing the Tithe creates for you are far, far worse than a disabled or malfunctioning vehicle. What your boss at work says because you're late from having taken the bus is important because we honor those who have authority over us, but God is the most important ultimate authority. Don't steal the Tithe.

Because we are a week in the hole, Tithe stealing is premeditated. We are a week in the hole because the Tithe is for blessings past. So, you are by faith sowing into the present because of the blessings of the past for the expected blessings of your future. See how God is multidimensional?

As the Tithe has seeded the transaction, who supplied the Tithe? God did. So, we owe Him again. That's why the Tithe is paid, but the offering is given. You plan to either pay, delay or steal the Tithe the week before. To fight the temptation you have to plan **not** to steal it. Use your willpower; will to Tithe.

And there's still more, God wants His Tithe to return to Him, ***not void.*** God has instructed His Word, His Tithe to go out, prosper accordingly, return and don't return without having done its job. We all could take a lesson here. It's somewhat similar to, *Go to your room, do your homework, and don't come out until it's done.* When you come out of your room, you have the report to show that you did your homework. You have a total of 10 homework pages because of the one page of questions you took into the room.

Jesus couldn't go back to Heaven until He finished His work, so I don't know why so many of us are lollygagging around the planet as if we have nothing to do, just passing time. In God, everything and everybody has something to do based on their spiritual gifts and natural abilities. Everything has a purpose and to praise the Lord is just a part of it. The Tithe has purpose, and it can't go back to God as the Tithe until it finishes its work.

When we agree with God and receive our increase, we call the 10% within every increase the Tithe. We pay the money back to God as the Tithe. If it is not sown, it is taken away by the Devourer. Once it's in the hands of the Devourer, it loses its Tithe power.

Recall, God gives seed to the sower and bread to the eater, (Isaiah 55:10). So, the entire $500 does not belong to you. Part of what you have is seed and the other part is bread. Ten percent of it is designated as the Tithe, 90% of it is for your sustenance, and that's a whole lot of bread. Some part of the 90% you can choose to sow as Offerings. We have 9X the Tithe as our *take*. That means that $450 out of the 500 belongs to us. Because the initial $50 is **God's money**. The $50 Tithe is the Word *disguised* as money that kicked off the whole cycle.

Since it is more blessed to give than to receive, and God is more blessed than we are if we are receiving money, it's because He **gave**. What did He give? Use of the Tithe for our prosperity. His Word--, the anointing over the Tithe for its power and authority to accomplish its purpose. Most of all, He gave the sacrificial Lamb, Jesus Christ. For that we show gratitude, not *greedy-tude*. You're getting paid, receiving money and increase legally as a tither, but you are a week in the hole because this process started out with something and **God supplied that something**. This is why we **owe** the Tithe. It is why the Tithes paid, but the offering is given.

Jesus said, ***It is more blessed to give than to receive,*** (Acts 20:35B). God, who is more blessed, starts off the process by sending out a Word which attracts 9X itself to itself. Then the entire harvest of 100% comes our way. We are harvesters when we receive and pick through what we reap, taking out the best 10% and giving it back to God. Even a farmer knows to pick out the best of the harvest for seed. By doing this, when we receive increase, we identify the best, the first, as the Tithe. We agree with God. God requires the Tithe of us, which He not only sanctifies and consecrates, He **confirms** that it is the Tithe and anoints it to continue working for us.

We love him because he first loved us, (John 4:19).

We are blessed being able to keep 9X the Tithe is a high blessing, but God is **more** blessed. We are behind God because He *first* loved us. He first gave to us. He is first and we follow His lead. That's why you should be grateful, cheerful and excited to come to church and pay God the Tithe that He first provided to us for our prosperity.

If you don't. You're working like the devil to be a ***voider*** of the Tithe when you avoid paying the Tithe. When this happens, the power and anointing of the Tithe in any and all other money in your possession is cancelled on your behalf.

Recall that even if the Word has to go through Hell, it's going to come back to God. God's Tithe goes through the Devil's hands every time a saint withholds it, and that's because the Devourer's job is to go get it, and he does.

We must do our part to be sure that doesn't happen, because God always gets His Word back. Where is Jesus, the Word? At the right hand of the Father. Case in point.

Who Are You?

The amount of Tithe that you pay signifies what level you attain to in the Kingdom and what God thinks of you as a channel of blessing. It speaks of your faithfulness, trustworthiness, love, discipline, and obedience to him. It speaks of position and relationship. It's not the title you appear to hold at your church, not the seat you sit in, but the Tithe speaks to God and man. Conversely, even if you have the most awesome title in the church because of your good works, if you're a non-tither, you are <u>not</u> what your title says you are.

I'm not just talking about titles such as Deacon, trustee, Minister, Praise Leader. Sometimes that title is simply saint or member. Saints tithe. Members of the Body of Christ tithe. *Members* of churches pay dues. Members of the Body Tithe; are you part of the Kingdom of God? Or are you just a name on the social society called the church roll? If you can't confirm that you are saint by being a tither, which is the most prevalent of church titles, there's no way you can affirm that you or anything else that God calls, whether of the fivefold ministry gifts, or positions within the church, including any rank higher than the entry level position of *seeker*.

All of us should appreciate being a partaker of the Divine Nature of God and should celebrate God for allowing it. You should be honored and well pleased to have a part in returning God's Word disguised is only money back to Him, or at least not being the reason why it got hijacked and went to the kingdom of the devil.

Your Tithe confirms your title in the Kingdom of God. It says two things. You agree with God, especially when it comes to money, and He agrees with you, especially when it comes to money and power.

What's the title without the power and authority that goes with it? Nothing. And He confirms that title that you believe you have in the Kingdom because you are a tither. It states the truth is in you and you are not a liar.

- Then give Him something extra because you love and worship Him--, an offering.
- If I want to know who you are in God, I'd look at your Tithes and your tithing record.
- Your Tithe is like your crown. It speaks of your steadfastness, diligence, consistency, faith, patience, and trust in God. It confirms your title in the Kingdom of God.

The 10 Commandments of the Tithe

The 10 commandments of Exodus 20:13-17 are for sinners; they are the very basics. The desire to do or not to do these commandments is the measure of the state of maturity of the soul. The ability to resist states the position of the will. How you behave when confronted with sin, How you respond when you encounter sin in others is metered on one end by discernment and judgment, and on the other end by compassion and the Fruits of the Spirit. The will of a man is one of the reflections of the spirit of the man. The will shows saints and sinners your inner life, identifying you as a saint or a sinner. You must master the 10 commandments. Soul prosperity is the beginning of success in life, but the Word says that soul prosperity and financial prosperity as well as health all go together, (3 John 2).

The Tithe reflects the 10 commandments. Whether and how you pay shows saints and sinners your inner life. If you continually have to go over the very basics of the faith, then you cannot move to the next level.

As we talk about money, we must apply the laws of God as well. The laws are the very basics, even as they apply to money. For you legalists, the Tithe is what sets sinners apart. A non tither is a Sinner. Under which Law of Moses? Lying. Stealing. Coveting, idolatry and adultery. (Exodus 2:3-17). I don't know if foolishness is a sin, but ignorance is, (Numbers 15:25), so I had to add that to the list.

Of all the people to rob, why God? Why would you pick the person who loves you the most but can also destroy you with the consuming fire? Why would you pick the pocket of the person who will know that you stole the Tithe before you even steal it? What sense does this make? That really speaks of boldness of the *spirit* that's in you, and the Spirit is not of God. It also speaks of the depravity of your soul. To steal the Tithe chronically and continually without conscience speaks of a lack of knowledge and soul prosperity.

But when you move from sin to obedience, you begin to learn more about the things of God, uncovering layers and layers of His love. Power, money, 9X the Tithe is God's gift to you for your life and godliness. It is Jehovah Jireh's plan to bless you, even in the presence of your enemies. It's a mighty gift for your obedience. It is the indicator of position and relationship. It signifies your title--, good and faithful servant.

The 10 Commandments of Tithing

Thou shalt not make money thy God, especially the Tithe. Thou shalt not commit idolatry. When you put anything before God, you exalt that thing above Him. When you put money before God, you commit idolatry. As a matter of fact, since the Church is to be the Bride of Christ, idolatry is as if we commit adultery, God has stated that He is a jealous God, further, you as a member of your local church, you compromise the entire Body of Christ.

... Or it is profitable for thee, that one of thy members should perish and not the whole body should be cast into hell, (Matthew 5:29).

Thou shall not pretend to tithe.

Statistics say that only 20% of those who profess Christ are tithers. Perhaps you don't know what a tither pays. A tither pays 10% of all his increase. Not just every now and again, but when he feels like it, but always in every time he receives any increase.

Too many can be caught filling out tithing envelopes or putting in tokens or a mere pittance.

Those who come up when the tithers are called forth in the service come up to give the *appearance* of being a tither. **Thou shalt not pretend to tithe**. Thou shalt not misname the Tithe as *only money*. The Tithe has power and anointing *only money* doesn't.

As we have discussed in previous chapters, *only money* is inanimate. It is inactive. *Only money* doesn't do much of anything for anybody except provide <u>now</u> things for today and tomorrow. If you want investment, security, and assurance that you'll have *enough*, you must not reduce the Tithe, which boasts of power and anointing to *only money* by spending it at the grocery store or the mall. You have to put the Tithe where it goes--, in the offering plate, so it will please God, work for you, and prosper you. And, so it will be kept out of the enemy's hand. As well as provide for your future.

Thou shalt not make any purchases before you pay the Tithe.

The Tithe is paid first, (Romans 11:16) says that if the first fruit be holy, then the lump is holy.. The first fruit is when you give all of your first to God, but the principle of the Tithe when sanctified, makes the *lump* holy. So when the 10% is blessed, consecrated and submitted to God, the rest of the money is blessed too. It goes further for you.

Remember the Tithe and keep it holy.

The Tithe is kept holy by returning it to God in a timely fashion. As you prosper, pay God His 10%.

Thou shalt not kill thine own prosperity. The method that God has put in place to bless you.

When you violate any spiritual law or principles of money, you hurt yourself more than you hurt God. God has gone to the effort of putting a system in place to bless you, keep you, even in the hostile world in which we live. Who in the world actually wants you to prosper? Few, really. The reality is many people are very greedy and covetous. When you steal, spend, or give the Tithe away instead of bringing it to the God, you kill your own prosperity and bring on the Curse of the Law.

It does hurt God because He takes pleasure in the prosperity of His servant. If you're not prospering, then you have not only stolen the money that was indicated as the Tithe, but you also have stolen pleasure from God. Since the joy of the Lord is your strength, (Nehemiah 8:10). You've really messed up. Don't wonder if you feel weak.

As a parent, you love to see your child happy and well provided for; God is no different than that about you.

In Malachi 3, God says not to rob Him. But when we rob God, we rob ourselves of benefit and provision, and we rob God of the **joy** of seeing us prosper. Don't you hate it when you're trying to bless your child, but they don't cooperate? So, you have to withhold that new bicycle or other gift from them. God doesn't want to withhold from you either.

Thou shalt not lie about the Tithe--, not the amount or the whereabouts.

Two of the most well-known characters in the New Testament were Ananias and Sapphira. They lied even without speaking about the amount of their Tithe. By bringing only what they wanted to give while leaving part of it at home. And they lied about the whereabouts of their Tithe. They pretended it was all there, that was all of it, but part of it was at home, between the mattress and the box springs. This is tied closely with pretending to tithe. It doesn't work. They both dropped dead. Is that what you want? Thou shall not covet the Tithe.

Don't covet thy neighbor's tithe.

Thou shalt not covet. The first step in stealing is having the *mind* to steal. After that, the plan to steal comes to mind, then the plan to steal to get away with it. Coveting is the first step in stealing.

In the New Testament, God says that the man who looks upon a woman with a lust has already sinned. When you look upon your Tithe or your neighbor's Tithe *with lust,* you may have already sinned. Beware, do not covet.

Honor the source of all thine increase--, God.

We honor God by keeping His commandments, obeying His laws, operating His principles, obeying His precepts, etcetera. One of the most obvious ways we honor God is with money. We pay God what is His and honor Him with what is ours. We pay God His Tithe, and we honor Him by giving our offerings. What about our offerings 30-, 60-, and 100-fold return? Isn't that greater than 9X? Yes, but you can't receive in the 30-fold, 60-fold, 100-fold return offering **until** you are a tither.

I'm pretty impressed that I can keep 9X the Tithe and still have plenty of increase for life and godliness. And after Tithing. Glory to God. You can move into the 30-, 60-, and 100-full blessings of God, but first things first, ***tithe***.

That makes 10 commandments of tithing. You may think of more.

Epilogue

I pray this book has enlightened you and set you free in the realm of the Tithe, and that it will cause you to prosper greatly and bring pleasure to God as He sits up high and looks down low at His good and faithful servant--, you.

In this book, we focused on the Tithe. This is not to say you should live by tithing only. You must give generous offerings as well. Bishop Don Mears of Evangel Cathedral, Upper Marlboro, MD, has challenged revelation on the 30-, 60-, and 100-fold return on offerings. I accepted the challenge hence, **Power Money. Nine Times the Tithe** and then the sequels, **The Fold**, **Name Your Seed**, **The Poor Attitudes of Money.** This series is about how to get returns on your Offerings and answers the 30, 60, and 100-fold question.

The mini book, **Do Not Orphan Your Seed** is excerpted entirely from **Name Your Seed**. To keep a record of your sowing, get the Sowing Journal.

Blessings.

Dr. Marlene Miles.

Christian books by this author

AK: Adventures of the Agape Kid

AMONG SOME THIEVES

Ancestral Powers

As My Soul Prospers

Behave

Churchzilla (Wanna-Be Bride of Christ)

The Coco-So-So Correct Show

Demonic Cobwebs

Demonic Time Bombs

Demons Hate Questions

Do Not Orphan Your Seed

Do Not Work for Money

Don't Refuse Me Lord

Every Evil Bird

Evil Touch

The FAT Demons

Fruit of the Womb: Prayers Against Barrenness, *Book 2*

got Money?

Let Me Have a Dollar's Worth

Living for the NOW of God

Lord, Help My Debt

Lose My Location

Made Perfect In Love

The Man Safari *(I'm Just Looking)*

Marriage Ed., *Rules of Engagement & Marriage*

Motherboard: *Key to Soul Prosperity*

My Life As A Slave

Name Your Seed

Plantation Souls

The Poor Attitudes of Money

Power Money: Nine Times the Tithe

The Power of Wealth

Prayers Against Barrenness, For Success in Business and Life, *Book 1*

Seasons of Grief

Seasons of War

Second Marriage, Third Marriage any Marriage

SOULS in Captivity

Soul Prosperity: Your Health & Your Wealth

The *spirit* of Poverty

This Is *NOT* That: How to Keep Demons from Coming at You

The Throne of Grace, *Courtroom Prayers*

Warfare Prayer Against Poverty

When the Devourer is Rebuked

The Wilderness Romance

Other Journals & Devotionals by this author:
The Cool of the Day – Journal
got HEALING? Verses for Life
got HOPE? Verses for Life
got WISDOM? Verses for Life
got GRACE? Verses for Life
got JOY? Verses for Life
got LOVE? Verses for Life
He Hears Us, Prayer Journal
I Have A Star, Dream Journal
I Have A Star, Guided Prayer Journal,
J'ai une Etoile, Journal des Reves
Let Her Dream, Dream Journal *in colors*
Men Shall Dream, Dream Journal,
My Favorite Prayers (in 4 styles)
My Sowing Journal
Tengo una Estrella, Diario de Sueños

Illustrated children's books by Dr. Miles

Big Dog (8-book series)

Do Not Say That to Me

Every Apple

Fluff the Clouds

I Love You All Over the World

Imma Dance

The Jump Rope

Kiss the Sun

The Masked Man

Not During a Pandemic

Push the Wind

Tangled Taffy

What If?

Wiggle, Wiggle; Giggle, Giggle

Worry About Yourself

You Did Not Say Goodbye to Me

www.ingramcontent.com/pod-product-compliance
Lightning Source LLC
Chambersburg PA
CBHW070853050426
42453CB00012B/2166